Spiral Dragon Dharma Gate

"To gain the wisdom contained in *Spiral Dragon Dharma Gate*, one would traditionally have had to journey to a remote cave in Tibet for teachings—teachings which you now hold here in print."
    Peter Mt. Shasta, author of *Apprentice to the Masters*

"*The Spiral Dragon Dharma Gate* is what is known as a terma or treasure teaching, which was received from Senton Dorje, a great master and a nun of the Nyingma tradition of Tibet, who was a reincarnation of the fierce yogini Machig Labdrön. Over the course of several years, Senton Dorje then gave this treasure of teachings and practices in mind-to-mind transmission to Master Quan, a Chinese master of many spiritual disciplines. These teachings were then brought to the USA, where Lama Johndennis Govert, an accomplished practitioner and fervent disciple of Master Quan, has passed on these pristine teachings to us today. How fortunate! This teaching and practice is aimed at achieving the highest level of spiritual awakening—supreme awareness in the primordial state of Ultimate Reality. A great treasure indeed."
    Luke Blue Eagle, author of
    First Nations Crystal Healing

"This splendid book literally blew me away! It shows you how to accelerate your path to enlightenment by uniting your body and mind through powerful exercises explained with perfect clarity."
    Clear Englebert, author of *Feng Shui for Real Estate*
    and *Feng Shui for Love & Money*

"Stagnation of movement and thought causes suffering. It's vital to adopt healthy practices and methods such as those described in this book, which can free the flow of energy within us, loosen our tight grip on concepts, and engender awareness of the mind-ground. The practices in *Spiral Dragon Dharma Gate* offer simple and effective ways to accomplish this."

Don Kimon Lightner, L.Ac.,
Herbalist and Acupuncturist

Spiral Dragon Dharma Gate

Six Key Tibetan Practices for Enlightenment

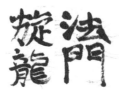

JOHNDENNIS GOVERT,
LAMA RANGDANG NAMKHA

Destiny Books
Rochester, Vermont

Destiny Books
One Park Street
Rochester, Vermont 05767
www.DestinyBooks.com

Text stock is SFI certified

Destiny Books is a division of Inner Traditions International

Copyright © 2025 by Johndennis Govert

All rights reserved. No part of this book may be reproduced or utilized in any form or by any means, electronic or mechanical, including photocopying, recording, or any information storage and retrieval system, without permission in writing from the publisher. No part of this book may be used or reproduced to train artificial intelligence technologies or systems.

Note to the reader: This book is intended as an informational guide. The remedies, approaches, and techniques described herein are meant to supplement, and not to be a substitute for, professional medical care or treatment. They should not be used to treat a serious ailment without prior consultation with a qualified health care professional.

Cataloging-in-Publication Data for this title is available from the Library of Congress

ISBN 979-8-88850-157-3 (print)
ISBN 979-8-88850-158-0 (ebook)

Printed and bound in the United States by Lake Book Manufacturing, LLC
The text stock is SFI certified. The Sustainable Forestry Initiative® program promotes sustainable forest management.

10 9 8 7 6 5 4 3 2 1

Text design and layout by Priscilla Harris Baker
This book was typeset in Garamond Premier Pro with FreightBig Pro, Gill Sans, Legacy Sans, Montserrat, and Sofia used as display typefaces

To send correspondence to the author of this book, mail a first-class letter to the author c/o Inner Traditions, One Park Street, Rochester, VT 05767, and we will forward the communication.

Scan the QR code and save 25% at InnerTraditions.com. Browse over 2,000 titles on spirituality, the occult, ancient mysteries, new science, holistic health, and natural medicine.

Contents

Acknowledgments — vii

Introduction to Spiral Dragon — 1

1 Spiral Dragon Dharma Gate Origins
The Treasure Revealed
by Khandro Senton Dorje — 13

2 Spiral Dragon Dynamics
Three Phases of Joyful Self-Actualizing — 24

3 Beginning Spiral Dragon
Relying upon Relaxation and Intuition — 33

4 Moving and Integrating Energy
Hands, Breath, and Thought — 45

5 Restoring Your Health and Energy
Recalling, Recharging, and
Rebalancing Qi Energy — 61

6 Creative Play and Progress
Rhythms of Spiral Dragon — 76

7 Refining Your Destiny
Signs in the Hands — 88

8   Mudra, Mantra, and Inner Transformation
Interconnections of Body, Breath, and Mind   102

9   Infinite Light Path of Bodhi Mind
Exploring the Limits of Intention   118

Epilogue
Dharma Unfolding Destiny   134

Appendix 1
Spiral Dragon Mantra Wisdom   139

Appendix 2
Spiral Dragon Exercise Sequences   153

Notes   161

Bibliography   162

Index   163

Acknowledgments

I have only been able to present Spiral Dragon to you because of the kindness of my teachers to whom I am deeply grateful, to Senton Dorje who discovered this treasure teaching and Master Guan-liang Quan who taught this path directly to me. I am grateful to all those students who wanted to learn Spiral Dragon and who have improved my teaching over the years with their quandaries and questions. I am further indebted to those of you who become inspired to activate the Spiral Dragon path to benefit yourselves and the world.

I extend my thanks to all who have given me insightful advice on how to present Spiral Dragon in a clear way. I especially want to thank my wife, Anita, for encouraging and supporting me to preserve the teachings of Spiral Dragon for posterity, and to review the copy as I produced it. I also want to acknowledge the encouragement I received from Master Quan's disciples who learned Spiral Dragon directly from him and were kind enough to listen and to advise me. I want to especially thank Hapi Hara for reviewing versions of the manuscript as it took gradual form as a book, and offering her valuable suggestions for improvements along the way. The images of the postures of Spiral Dragon are as important as the written instruction, and I thank Kaleigh Brown for her photography and skills in image processing to produce the illustrations that enliven the text.

I also am very grateful to Inner Traditions and Destiny Books for being an essential link in making Spiral Dragon available to a wide audience. Specifically, I want to thank Jon Graham and Jeanie Levitan for bringing Spiral Dragon forward for many to benefit. I thank Emilia Cataldo, Courtney Jenkins, Jodi Shaw, and the entire editorial staff for encouraging a more perfect manuscript and helping craft the book into an excellent presentation. I very much appreciate Chris Cappelluti, Manzanita Carpenter Sanz, Ashley Kolesnik, Rob Meadows, and the Inner Traditions marketing staff who are getting this book into the hands of those who need it. Finally, the unfathomable web of causes and effects that led to this book appearing from the depths of the cosmos are so vast they can only be regarded as an infinite and perfect blessing. Thank you all.

Introduction to Spiral Dragon

Q Doesn't it seem like in each generation now people are becoming duller and less intelligent?

A It doesn't just seem that way, it is that way! Our current generation has reached the critical threshold of collective ignorance. Either humans will devolve into a long cycle of widespread stupidity and bondage, or they will arise into the light of awakening, greater wisdom, happiness, and spiritual brilliance. Spiral Dragon is an important practice to accelerate this transformation personally and collectively now.

This spontaneous question and answer arose between a student and Master Guan-liang Quan during a Spiral Dragon practice and teaching session in 1990. He went on to state that we need each other to master the gifts, skills, and great potentials we are born with so that we can transform this world to create the positive future alternative. And quickly. The activated excellence of everyone is necessary now which is why this treasure teaching has come forward to help each person discover, cultivate, and contribute their unique excellence. Each person has a choice of a positive destiny, but each has to engage that destiny to create satisfying self-benefit as well as incalculably great universal benefit. This is an urgent matter and the reason for this Spiral Dragon book.

2   Introduction to Spiral Dragon

The symbolic urgent reason for Spiral Dragon.

I was introduced to Master Quan and Spiral Dragon in the summer of 1989. Master Quan had arrived in Seattle shortly after the Beijing, Tiananmen Square riots that occurred from mid-April to early June of that year. How Master Quan managed to arrange for extended travel in order to teach healing and Spiral Dragon in the United States at that time of critical People's Republic of China (PRC) turmoil was an astounding improbability. In July, I too had just relocated back to Seattle after five years in the Los Angeles area. It was another space and time improbability because everything I had ever studied or experienced was important for this next step. Within a month I was driving Master Quan to teach Spiral Dragon classes at the Northwest Institute of Acupuncture and Oriental Medicine. By the fall of 1989, Master Quan had begun teaching regular weekly classes open to the public at large.

What was astounding to me was the profound results that flowed from the simplicity and ease of practicing Spiral Dragon, both the energy exercises and meditation. Had I not learned and practiced taiji, qi gong, and other energy systems, I would have had no venerable standards for comparison to see the ease of Spiral Dragon. Also, because I had practiced Zen and Tibetan Buddhist meditation extensively, I was able to appreciate that Spiral Dragon meditation is the easier essence of these meditations. Even though I wished I had found Spiral Dragon much sooner, I realized that I needed to practice the traditional way these self-cultivation disciplines are taught in order to recognize Spiral Dragon as their original center. This book is my opportunity to offer you a way to ease and accelerate your spiritual practices from the authentic and profound root. I will present Spiral Dragon to you from a number of interconnecting perspectives. My main concern is for you to easily learn this liberating system of body, energy, and mind cultivation. I want to inspire positive motivation for you to try Spiral Dragon with enthusiasm.

This introduction and chapters two and three will give you a context for what Spiral Dragon is and is not. In chapters three, four, and five I will present the main wisdom sequence and self-healing exercises which Master Quan proved to himself created the greatest, practical acceleration to realizing enlightenment for his disciples and students. Beginning at chapter five, we will also consider how to apply Spiral Dragon teachings to restore our health and energy. Even though the healing techniques we will explore are not part of the main sequence of Spiral Dragon, we all need to continually adjust our health and life force energy, especially after struggling through the 2020 pandemic. Spiral Dragon contains a set of mantras and a targeted set of exercises to resolve acute and chronic health conditions that interfere with productively accomplishing our intentions and enjoying life every day.

In chapter six, after learning Spiral Dragon exercises individually, we consider how to combine them into the rhythm of a session. This chapter will be more about launching the trajectory of your Spiral Dragon experience. Here I will convey the guidance that Master Quan gave to answer common student questions asked over the course of years. While the how-to chapters give you an idea of what experiences you will have right away, this gives you a sense of how Spiral Dragon can transform your life positively over weeks, months and seasons. Finally, I give some examples of how Master Quan applied the skills he acquired in practicing Spiral Dragon to solve planet-scale problems. Although we won't be able to operate to improve the world effectively and immediately, it's important to see how a master was able to apply Spiral Dragon. This is not about a parade of fantastic horizons; on many occasions Master Quan discussed with his students how they could use Spiral Dragon to develop extraordinary accomplishments, including navigation of critical global threats.

After you have learned the basic Spiral Dragon exercises, applied them to your health, and integrated them into regular practice, you can begin extending Spiral Dragon directly to develop your potentials. Chapter seven presents specific postures and exercises that provide ways to investigate the worlds around you. It is a more open discussion, because each person has different, urgent questions about the universe they want to explore and resolve. Spiral Dragon practice will magnetize your destiny so that you become very confident of the nature of your life's work. This chapter presents techniques to tune your intuition and spontaneously open new levels of life skills that fulfill your reason for being here on Earth now.

Parallel to Spiral Dragon, Master Quan taught how to use mantras and mudras to increase the effectiveness of the entire system. Chapter eight discusses the ancient science of sound vibrations and how you can apply these to improve your health, insight, and intuition. Appendix 1 adds more information about how to pronounce, chant, and use mantras for specific purposes. It also organizes all the mantras in the whole book in one place. The second topic, mudras, is often defined as hand gestures. Mudras are ways of holding your hands and body to induce positive flows of energy to create greater health, peace, inspiration, and abilities of body and mind. Mantras and mudras are part of the greater system of Spiral Dragon.

Chapter nine explores the limits of intention both negative and positive. Through harnessing infinite compassion, you can generate open and undefeatable intention. If you are interested in practicing Spiral Dragon in the context of Buddhism, we discuss Master Quan's eight-word core dharma that can bring balance and happiness into our lives and the lives of others. The chapter concludes by considering how you will know you have engaged Spiral Dragon successfully both in the short and long runs. Attentively watching the signs of Spiral Dragon dynamics arise from moment to moment and season to season is the basis for continuing progress, motivation, and joy.

First, let me describe what Spiral Dragon is, or more formally, what Spiral Dragon Dharma Gate is. For that, let's start with the fifty-thousand-foot overview. Anyone who undertakes spiritual practice has a very wide choice of techniques to try. Each person needs to find a practice that especially resonates with them, but all practices fall broadly into two approaches: the path of method and the path of liberation. The path of method precisely defines the yogic process and is characterized by a graduated series of practices from foundational to advanced. These practices require a more technical understanding of each practice, and, how each one fits into the overall strategy of sequenced practices in order to complete the path. There are established criteria for judging whether you have qualified to move forward, have barely passed, or have mastered each practice phase. The advantage of the path of method is that it outlines and measures the effort required to create spiritual transformation. This path recognizes individual differences, so it is not mechanistic. Teachers and gurus who have mastered a part or the entire series of practices can tell when a student has achieved a transformative step or not. Teachers can change the practice to match the potential and progress of the student in dynamic response. The overall intention of the path of method practices is enlightenment, but each specific practice has its own phase intention and goal.

By contrast, the path of liberation has the primary intention of enlightenment or liberation. Each liberation practice elaborates on the ability to recognize and rest your mind in its original nature. This very first practice accomplishes the path holistically. Other liberation practices are aimed at gaining greater confidence, understanding, and ease in being and radiating enlightened mind whether engaged in quiet contemplation or dynamic movement. In this approach, you do not gradually improve yourself until you achieve the pinnacle of perfection. Instead, the main practice points out that you are and have been completely enlightened before the beginning of time. Additional practices are designed to clarify and catalyze the recognition of your own primordial enlightened nature. In this teaching, there is no fundamental difference between Buddhas or Awakened Ones and ordinary sentient beings. Zen Master Hakuin Ekaku expresses this in the first lines of *Zazen Wasan*, or *Song of Meditation*:

> *All beings from the very beginning are Buddhas*
> *It is like water and ice:*
> *Apart from water, no ice,*
> *Outside living beings, no Buddhas.*[1]

The advantage of the path of method is that you can gauge your progress along the way to enlightenment. There are mileposts on land and buoys at sea. The two disadvantages of the method path are that the seeker can become more reliant on the external directions and less reliant on intuition and the arising of fundamental wisdom from within. The main disadvantage, however, is that to complete the ultimate goal of profound awakening, you have to abandon the path of method entirely. Once you are sure that you have prepared as much as possible, the method path disappears in the borderless sky and only the path of liberation remains as the completion process. Similarly, even though the intent of the path of liberation is profound enlightenment, that intent creates its own impasse requiring that even that great intention must be abandoned for uncontrived liberation to arise. The basis for the liberation path is recognizing spontaneous awakening moment by moment. Spontaneous awareness is the natural condition. Sometimes this awareness, which is complete in itself, simply rests in itself. Sometimes the dynamic of awareness presents you with insights and approaches to resolve conditions that arise in everyday life. Spiral Dragon Dharma Gate is primarily the discovery and expression of your unique potential on the path of liberation. At this point, let's explore

DNA double spiral molecule.

the characteristics of this practice which are concentrated in the meanings of spiral, dragon, dharma, and gate.

Spiral, or *xuan*² (旋) in Chinese,* describes this spiritual practice as nonlinear, resonating instead with the spiral motions of nature at every scale. Most notably at a nanometer scale (one-billionth of a meter), our biology activates through the double helix structure of human DNA. At the solar system level, as the sun moves through space at approximately 500,000 miles per hour, the planets in their orbits actually follow along on spiral paths. At greater size scales measured in light years, many galaxies are organized in and move as spiral structures like our own Milky Way. Movement in spirals is the path for life growth. It is described by the mathematics of the Fibonacci number sequence and is known also as the golden mean. For example, trees and sea shells grow in spirals. This is important because the energy of Spiral Dragon also flows in spirals through the body and through space and time. This is an altogether different flow pattern from qi energy which by contrast moves along and through the acupuncture meridians in a more linear pattern.

---

*Throughout the book, Chinese words are transcribed in Roman letters in Pinyin format. The superscript number refers to tones one through four to indicate Mandarin pronunciation.

Messier 83 is a spiral galaxy showing scatterings of
bright stars and thick dust.
Credit: NASA / ESA / the Hubble Heritage Team / STScI /
AURA / William Blair, Johns Hopkins University

At this point, it makes sense to examine the practices of qi gong (氣 功), which outwardly resemble Spiral Dragon in form, but are different in intent and result. Qi has been described as "matter on the verge of becoming energy, or energy at the point of materializing."[2] A good emphasis meaning for qi is: "Life is the proliferation of Qi, death is its dissolution."[3] Qi has been translated as life force or life energy that flows along body pathways that have been identified for thousands of years as acupuncture meridians in Traditional Chinese Medicine (TCM). In the Daoist yoga of China and yogas of India and Tibet, qi flow is recognized as occurring in more minor flows within the body plane and through thousands of channels outside the body in the aura. In TCM, more formally this system of qi channels is called *jing*[1] *luo*[4]. The *jing* channels are twelve vertical channels right and left that connect the body's organs. A central yin channel in front and central yang channel at the back make a total of fourteen types of main *jing* channels. The *luo* channels are seven minor horizontal flow channels. The harmonic number of qi flow channels is twenty-one, which will be important in the actual Spiral Dragon practice described later. There are acupuncture points along these channels where the electrical potential measures higher than at other locations on the body or along acupuncture meridians.[4] These points can be identified objectively, but whether in qi gong or Spiral Dragon, it is more important to encounter qi and its flow subjectively through your internal senses of seeing, hearing, and feeling.

The phenomenon of qi practice in qi gong is a linear display. For instance, if you apply the power of qi force with a martial-arts move to push someone away, that person will be pushed in a straight line, not in a full spiral nor even a partial arc. This linearity is true also of other applications of qi gong with the six primary practice intentions to develop:

1. Martial arts skills
2. Abilities to heal self or others
3. Supernormal powers
4. Enhanced artistic skills
5. Greater mind and psychic abilities
6. Yogic and spiritual self-cultivation

These primary practice intentions coupled with qi energy activate different ranges of energy, each with unique, practical potentials. The intention of Spiral Dragon is complete enlightenment, fully awake and at ease in the natural state. This means that although some qi gong practices may create contrived ways that rewire the subtle body to achieve particular results, Spiral Dragon, by contrast, opens your entire being naturally in an uncontrived return to the awakened state. It unravels each person's particular twist of qi and karma in a self-arising, backward sequence that is uniquely perfect for each person.

The second characteristic of Spiral Dragon is *dragon* (龍) which has many shades of meaning. First, the dragon is the fifth zodiac sign of Chinese astrology and is associated with the emperor just as the fifth sign of Leo is associated with kings and queens. This implies that Spiral

Dragon is a raja or royal practice that restores the sovereignty of the enlightened mind as rightful ruler of human experience. Second, the dragon is a being living between heaven and Earth and is associated with lightning, thunder, and rain. The powerful dragon brings great transformation to the landscape just as Spiral Dragon powerfully transforms us. Third, dragons are great, mysterious, spiritual, and unpredictably independent. The dragon follows its own nature despite social conventions and appearances. This description, whether the dragon is connected to water or sky, applies equally to the path of Spiral Dragon. Fourth, both dragon types guard great wealth. In fact, the dragon race is the wealthiest race of beings throughout all the worlds on Mount Meru, the cosmic mountain. This great wealth is both material and spiritual. Sky dragons are often depicted grasping a fiery pearl, the great *chintamani* or wish-fulfilling gem. Fifth, in Buddhism, sky dragons are associated with higher teachings of internal transformation and enlightenment. Each eon, before a great Buddha descends to Earth to renew the teachings of enlightenment, that Buddha-to-be first appears in a heaven of the high dragons who impart the most complete and sublime teachings of awakening. Spiral Dragon creates a living connection to the profound dragon teachers of the supreme dharma realm.

The third characteristic of Spiral Dragon is *dharma* which also has a wide range of pertinent meanings. The most applicable meaning of dharma is the set of teachings and practices that uncover enlightenment. When Buddhism was transmitted from India to China, the Sanskrit word, dharma, was translated as *fa*[3] using the Chinese ideograph 法. The lefthand side of the character is the radical or root symbol for water. On the right is the word for going, leaving, or departing. It can also mean the passing of time. It can imply time flow, or the flow of events. This translation of dharma, as in the original Sanskrit, also refers to law, but especially natural law, or the laws of nature. This is the word in Spiral Dragon Dharma Gate that points to the deep purpose of the practice as enlightenment. It identifies it as a Buddhist or awakening practice with that ultimate aim and result. It does not imply a need to believe in Buddhism because it is an experiential flow to transform yourself and the depth of your own heart and mind. In fact, you can practice Spiral Dragon in the context of Buddhism and its many other practices, or you may approach it as the path that develops your own personal dharma. In this sense, dharma refers to destiny, to the very reason that you embodied on Earth to pursue your root purpose in this lifetime. Whether you undertake Spiral Dragon to awaken completely, to discover and develop your true purpose, or to realize both intentions, it is entirely open to you. In this sense, Spiral Dragon is part of the path of liberation leading to enlightenment, and/or part of the path of method developing your destiny for the great benefit of sentient beings throughout all space in these critically transitional times.

The final characteristic of Spiral Dragon Dharma is *gate* which indicates it is a *whole system*. The actual word, *men*[3], written with the character 門, translates as gate, door, or entry. In the modern era of computers and management organization, this term has been extended to refer also to systems. The title of the book uses gate rather than system to show that Spiral Dragon serves as an entrance to another realm of being that is present constantly, but not often accessed. The combination of dharma and system affirm that Spiral Dragon is a complete path in and of itself to realize enlightenment. It does not require other Buddhist or spiritual practices in order to be effective ultimately. This is not to say that you cannot combine your regime of Buddhist, yogic, or other spiritual practices with Spiral Dragon. What you will find is that Spiral Dragon practice accelerates the experiences of your other practices so that they integrate naturally into your path of awakening.

A characteristic not in the name of Spiral Dragon Dharma Gate is the root of deep relaxation that flows to create powerful transformation. Spiral Dragon can be practiced from a standing or sitting posture, but either position requires the spine to be an upright and vertical connector of heaven and Earth energies. The relaxation exercise begins every session of Spiral Dragon and is an integral part of the entire practice. As we allow our bodies, emotions, and thoughts to relax, we allow our personal sharpness to untangle as we let go of attachments, preoccupations, and obsessions. We release pain and discomfort on every level to allow ourselves to resonate more perfectly with universal energy flows which are continually in play. Deep relaxation disperses distraction and opens up the greater extent of the present moment so that our aversions and expectations fall away and we naturally become openly aware in this moment. I'll conclude this chapter with another question-and-answer exchange between a student and Master Quan:

"You said that the whole basis of enlightenment is relaxation."

Yes!

"You said that if we can relax completely, we will become fully enlightened from that alone."

Yes!

"So, I could go home, practice perfect relaxation, and experience complete enlightenment."

You could, but you won't.

1

Spiral Dragon Dharma Gate Origins
The Treasure Revealed
by Khandro Senton Dorje

The value of dharma is that it works to awaken us completely to the spontaneous presence and flow of wisdom in our lives. It is not a monolithic message pointing everyone in the exact same direction. Since we each begin with a unique blend of karmas and experiences, it is the apparent blend of harmonies, dysfunctions, and potentials that create the life basis we each engage. This is what Buddha referred to as "84,000 dharmas." This is a large, sacred number symbolic of a very wide variety of human types, each with a particular path to enlightenment. Of the 84,000 dharma paths, only a few are optimally suited for each type of practitioner. After making a commitment to enlightenment, the next step is to find the circumstances and path that resonate most closely with your awakening core.

Within Buddhist teaching there are a great many teachings and methods that practitioners over several millennia have verified as leading to the fruit of enlightenment. Many of the teachings arise from the original instructions of the historical Buddha passed down and adapted to each generation by the realized gurus of the era. Many of these gurus wrote commentaries or simply instructed and coached their disciples. Another type of teaching known as *terma* or treasure teaching also arose in tantric Tibetan Buddhism. These treasure teachings are dependent on a guru with the karma to find sacred objects buried in the Earth, physically hidden texts, or teachings embedded in the guru's own mind stream. After discovery, the *terton*, or treasure revealer, decoded the new teachings from symbols to words, practices, and spontaneous wisdom, and then practiced the revealed dharma personally. Usually after many years of practice, the guru would know when and to whom to pass the precious teaching. Spiral Dragon Dharma Gate is a terma within the Tibetan Buddhist tradition of the Nyingma or ancient order of translations. The treasure revealer was Khandro Senton Dorje who encountered this teaching and practiced it during a thirteen-year solitary retreat in a cave in the area of Kumbum monastery in the Amdo region of Tibet.

The biography of Senton Dorje is minimal in personal detail, almost what one would expect from a highly realized yogini. Her disciples did not know her birth date nor much personal information beyond what they could observe directly for themselves. She reported that her dharma life formally began at eighteen years when she became a Buddhist. Though she was Chinese, she immediately undertook a pilgrimage to Tibet to learn and practice tantric Buddhism, eventually becoming a master in the Nyingma tradition. She entered Kumbun monastery as a nun, then at some point retired to a cave many miles away in the vicinity of Kumbun. It was during her thirteen-year cave retreat that she discovered and practiced Spiral Dragon Dharma Gate, attaining the fruition of profound enlightenment in that place. What I know of Senton Dorje I learned from my guru, Master Guan-liang Quan, who is my sole source of her biography. I will jump to his biography for a moment which includes how he met Senton Dorje, learned Spiral Dragon, and perfected it.

Master Quan was born in Shanghai on November 18, 1931, on the day of Medicine Buddha in the year of the Iron Sheep. His father was a teacher and practitioner of Traditional Chinese Medicine (TCM), including acupuncture and herbology, qi gong, and the martial arts. Master Quan learned and assiduously practiced these disciplines from early childhood. He also studied Daoist self-cultivation and yoga practices from childhood. At the time of his birth, Shanghai was a bustling international port city where the cultures of the world intermingled freely. Master Quan attended an international school operated by German missionaries where he began learning the German language in which he would later become fluent. The Second Sino-Japanese War began in 1937 in which Japan invaded much of China, controlling and continually occupying major cities including Shanghai until the end of World War II. After the wars, Master Quan studied chemistry professionally and became a translator of many German chemical texts and studies into Chinese.

At some time in mid-1970s, Master Quan lived with his mother as his father had died. In that era, the People's Republic of China (PRC) initially suppressed all religious practices, so Master Quan secretly practiced Daoism but only could openly practice qi gong as a healing modality which was an officially recognized component of the PRC's health care system that combined modern Western medicine and TCM. By then, Master Quan was a well-regarded and well-known qi gong master who regularly participated in state sponsored conferences professionally investigating and discussing the role of qi gong in recovering and maintaining health. The regional and national conferences Master Quan attended afforded him the opportunity to openly explore the more subtle aspects of healing with masters from Buddhist, Daoist, Confucian, scientific, and modern schools of qi gong practice. In secret, these masters were able to confer and collaborate with one another about topics of inner transformation which the PRC considered religious and subject to censorship and callous suppression. These national treasure level masters were able to share the yogic skills they had developed and were experimenting across all fields of human endeavor.

When home in Shanghai, Master Quan's personal routine was to practice for most of the night. Since Shanghai homes were heated largely by burning charcoal, carbon monoxide poisoning was a common health hazard leading to possible death from charcoal smoke. His interest in staying up most of the night was to ensure that his mother could sleep comfortably and not be exposed to the risk of carbon monoxide poisoning. One night during practice with his eyes closed, he sensed a presence in the room. When he opened his eyes, he saw a woman standing in front of him, physically present in the room. He knew he had locked all the doors before practicing and had heard no one enter. This woman was Khandro Senton Dorje.

Senton Dorje immediately began to show Master Quan a number of postures and movements and silently bade him to follow along. At some point after the lesson, she disappeared from sight. She did not show up again for a month, but did reappear and taught him more. This instruction went on periodically for months with nothing spoken. One night she looked intensely at Master Quan and said: "You are my only disciple!" The lessons, with the sudden appearance and disappearance of Senton Dorje, continued but with the addition of sparse conversations. She revealed that this practice system, though resembling qi gong, was Spiral Dragon Dharma Gate, which had been revealed to her years earlier in retreat in the caves around Kumbun monastery. In addition to Spiral Dragon, Senton Dorje instructed Master Quan in the practices of Nyingma and other traditions of Tibetan Buddhism which took place over subsequent years at various places in China. What follows is the little that Master Quan learned of her over the years until her death in the late 1980s.

Khandro Senton Dorje remembered her past lives and disclosed to Master Quan that she was a reincarnation of Machig Labdron, an eleventh-century, famous and realized Tibetan Buddhist female master. The dharma system she revealed and practiced in that lifetime is known as *Chod* or cutting through the ego. All of tantric Buddhism arose in India and was transmitted to Tibet starting in the eighth century. Machig's Chod practice, however, is the only tantric Buddhist teaching system that originated in Tibet and was transmitted back to India and other Asian Buddhist communities. Like Machig, Senton Dorje practiced as she wandered across Tibet and China. During times when

Spiral Dragon Dharma Gate Origins   ⁕   17

Fig. 1.1. The only surviving photo of Senton Dorje from Master Quan's collection.

the PRC aggressively restricted the practice of all religions, especially Buddhism, Senton Dorje came under surveillance and attack. At one point, the Red Guard surrounded a house in which they knew she was staying with the intent of capturing or killing her. When they broke into the house, Senton Dorje unexpectedly was not there. Through her awareness and yogic accomplishments, she was able to roam freely, to teach and care for disciples, students, and those who needed her help throughout her life despite the political climate.

In September of 1998, I accompanied Master Quan and several other disciples to search out greater knowledge of Senton Dorje. Our pilgrimage took us to Kumbun monastery near Xining, China, formerly Amdo, Tibet, but currently administered by the PRC as Qinghai province. Senton Dorje's practice at Kumbun was one of the few biographical details of her life that had enough specificity to check. Along the way to and from Chengdu to Lanzhou and Xining, as well as later in Lhasa, we met Tibetan Buddhist masters of the Gelugpa, Kagyu, and Nyingma sects. For the moment, I will defer this topic, but address it later in this chapter.

At Kumbun, also known as Ta^{3}er^{3}si^4 (塔爾寺) in Chinese, Master Quan hoped to speak with monastics who either knew Senton Dorje personally or knew of her practice there. He was hoping to learn any more facts about her, but especially wanted to find where her retreat cave might be located. After some initial introductions and conversations, Master Quan learned of a resident monk who might know. Since I am fluent neither in Chinese nor Tibetan, I was left in a garden to meditate while the group went in search of the monk. I only knew that I was in a pleasant but unknown large, treed garden. Master Quan instructed me to watch and meditate until our party returned with more information. Over an hour later, Master Quan and his Chinese disciples returned with the resident monk who knew the way and agreed to guide our driver to Senton Dorje's cave. Before we left, Master Quan asked me to report what I experienced. I was distracted by subtle perceptions of banners flying in most of the trees. I tried to determine the type of writing on the banners which was difficult as the banners constantly billowed in an astral wind. It was neither Chinese characters nor Tibetan script. It also didn't look like any of the Sanskrit scripts I knew. I thought I might be looking at *dakini* script though I had not been introduced to it before. In any event, I couldn't decode the script nor perceive a message. It was enough of an omen that I discovered the banners were in dakini language. At Kumbun monastery, the serene garden in which I meditated was known as the Dakini Garden. What is relevant is that in the Tibetan terma treasure tradition, new practices are often guarded by and revealed by the dakinis.*

We drove through the countryside with the fields full of standing sheaves of harvested grains and hay on the way toward the foothills. When we arrived, we found that the cave of Senton Dorje's retreat had been converted into a shrine and that a resident monk was practicing, living, and teaching there while tending the holy site. See Figures 1.2 and 1.3 below.

We all entered the cave, and each of us individually made prostrations and an incense offering. We meditated in silence for some time during which Master Quan made a very palpable mind-to-mind connection with his dear guru, Senton Dorje. Telepathically, he also received

---

*One of the ways that an Earth- or material-based treasure teaching is revealed is that the terton or revealer may discover a terse script on yellow paper in dakini writing. It is neither a letter- based nor syllable-based system conveying sounds in writing; rather, dakini script conveys symbols. The terton who reads the script immediately translates the symbols into conventional written language. Then later, inexplicably, the script disappears, leaving the paper blank.

Spiral Dragon Dharma Gate Origins   19

Fig. 1.2. The reconstructed entrance to Senton Dorje's original retreat cave near Xining, Qinghai province, PRC.

Fig. 1.3. In front of Senton Dorje's cave, from left to right: monk from Kumbun who guided us, the resident monk who tended Senton Dorje's retreat cave, and Master Quan.

instructions in higher level tantric yoga practices which brought him great joy and ineffable peace. During his discipleship, he met with Senton Dorje only a handful of times. He learned that she had very few serious students she considered disciples. Mostly she communicated her teachings by feelings of movement and telepathy, speaking very seldom. Earlier, on the train from Lanzhou to Xining, Master Quan taught us an advanced Green Tara practice from Machig Labdron's Chod tradition. When I asked for his guidance to teach me this practice step by step, he said: "I didn't learn it that way. When Senton Dorje taught me practices, I learned everything at once, not gradually. If you viewed us sitting in the same room when she transmitted the Green Tara practice, you would see a Green Tara image above her head. When she completed the transmission, you would see the exact same Green Tara image above my head. It was a complete information and experience transfer like copying a computer file from mind to mind."

An important aspect of the pilgrimage to the place of Spiral Dragon's origin was meeting a number of Tibetan Buddhist masters from the Gelug, Kagyu, and Nyingma sub-traditions as we traveled through Qinghai and Gansu provinces and to the city of Lhasa. Discussions with them affirmed that Senton Dorje was indeed a reincarnation of the fierce yogini, Machig Labdron, and that Spiral Dragon is reliable terma in the tradition of the treasure practice discoveries from the time of Padmasambhava to the present.* They came to this conclusion after listening to Master Quan's story of his training and after experiencing his healing abilities. They also enthusiastically examined the photos shown below as Figures 1.4 and 1.5. This came about because Master Quan traveled with about five photos in his front shirt pocket; only two

---

*Padmasambhava hid fresh and authentic dharma practices to resonate more fully with future enlightenment seekers especially as the world at large would and has become more materially focused to the detriment of true happiness and natural wisdom. Padmasambhava hid these as Earth treasures and in the mind streams of disciples. Khandro Senton Dorje's recognized Spiral Dragon Dharma Gate arising from her mind stream. I believe that she was inspired by psychically reading the dakini script banners aloft in the Dakini Garden of Kumbun Monastery. She spent thirteen years in solitary retreat to realize and practice Spiral Dragon fully before teaching it to anyone else.

of the most unusual ones are presented here. As we talked with each of the tantric masters we met, he would present the photos to them for their examination and comment. Let me explain these images.

In February of 1994, Master Quan traveled to Phoenix, Arizona, to dedicate Daikakuji, Great Enlightenment Temple, which I had founded. During the weekend, he taught Spiral Dragon directly to students who wanted to learn. Then on Sunday afternoon, he performed the ritual of opening the temple and connecting our teaching with the long, living Buddhist practice lineage. One of the Temple students who was an artist and photographer took the photos you see of the event. She took the photos with a good quality film camera with a flash. The photos below look hazy and double exposed, but the odd thing is that other photos taken that same day on the same film roll were crystal clear and properly lit both before and after the images you see with the strange spiral lights. In the altar room where the dedication ceremony occurred, there were no skylights or windows. In Figure 1.4, you can see a circling light stream above the altar where there was a statue of the Medicine Buddha.

Fig. 1.4. Master Quan (standing left) and author (standing right) amid unusual light display at the 1994 dedication of Dakaikuji Temple in Phoenix, Arizona.

Fig. 1.5. Master Quan (standing left) and author (standing right) in a rain of spiral lights at the 1994 dedication of Dakaikuji Temple in Phoenix, Arizona.

Figure 1.5 shows an unusual display of spiral lights. It was these photos of ritually invoked light phenomena that impressed the masters we met. The pilgrimage to Senton Dorje's cave and teachings from monks, gurus, and Master Quan along the way opened a deeper set of interconnections for Spiral Dragon to enter the world more fully. Several weeks after we had returned home, I asked Master Quan whether he now had realized a complete understanding of Spiral Dragon. (Ironically, his surname of Quan[2] [全] in Chinese means complete, whole, perfect, or entire.) His answer surprised me. He said that Senton Dorje had introduced him to Spiral Dragon, but had not explained it in any depth beyond demonstrating how to practice. It had become his life's dharma investigating what the implications and connections of Spiral Dragon are not only to Buddhist dharma, but to Daoism, western science, TCM, and other systems of inner transformation as well. Master Quan had received Senton Dorje's mind seal of approval as a master guru of Spiral Dragon in the very early 1980s. Before her death, in a meeting in April of 1983, he also received her blessing to teach her entire Nyingma dharma lineage. After this recent sacred journey, he realized his dynamic mastery of Spiral Dragon and its applications had indeed become complete. I asked him when his certainty occurred. He replied that it was when he had seen a particular *thangka** image of Machig Labdron that I had given to him. In that image she was standing in a dance posture with her hands in different mudras. During his own practice the very same posture and hand mudras spontaneously arose and he practiced that way for many months until he stabilized his Bodhisattva mind.

---

*A Tibetan Buddhist painting often done with gem and mineral pigments on cotton, or as a silk appliqué, usually depicting a Buddhist deity, scene, or mandala.

2

Spiral Dragon Dynamics
Three Phases of Joyful Self-Actualizing

The next chapter will describe how to actually practice the six main exercises of Spiral Dragon. While the postures at first may feel unfamiliar in the sequence in which they are arranged, each of the postures and movements are ones you've done in your life. Spiral Dragon movements are uncontrived and arise quite naturally. The basic sequence is very simple, powerful, and at the same time unfolds an easy set of essential body, energy, and mind integration. The profound mystery is how a seemingly simple practice can catalyze and harmonize all your fragments together so you realize happiness and your ultimate spiritual potential. What we consider here is the common basics of energy practices, their goals, and how they unfold in different systems compared with Spiral Dragon.

In many Asian systems of spiritual practice and inner cultivation, an essential part of the process is transforming your energy body so it vibrates at a higher frequency. This step makes it possible for deep and profound awareness to arise easily and to synergize with all your other inner transformation practices. Without this preparation, it is difficult to catalyze a significant shift out of the limits of our ordinary patterns, preferences, and views. The spark of life needs to burn with sufficient intensity to ignite the basis for higher order consciousness to emerge and establish itself. Normally, when this life spark fires, it produces bursts of short-term activity, awareness, and integration. Watching it work even once demonstrates that we can vibrate in a higher order, but need to establish that higher state of our being stably for the long-term. When greater energy is available, people naturally engage in life more actively and creatively. There are many reasons why this is the case, but let us consider three.

In Chinese metaphysics, reflected in TCM as well as Tibetan medicine, there are five elements. We discussed the jing luo system of meridians in the introduction. In TCM, the six pairs of meridians that mirror on the right and left sides of the body are connected to five elemental sets of yin and yang organs. With six meridian pairs available and only five elements to correspond, it means one element is repeated. You might guess the water element is repeated because of the high percentage of water comprising our bodies. Rather, it is fire that is the repeated element which flows through four instead of two meridians. Humans incorporate more fire not just into our physical bodies, but also into our energy meridians, ethereal bodies, and other subtle structures. Whether physical or subtle, we need to activate increased, sustained, balanced, fiery energy to function at high levels harmoniously.

In the introduction, we also discussed the subtle flow patterns of qi energy inside and outside the body plane. While there are twenty-one flows within the body, there are magnitudes of greater flows outside the body. Depending on the practice tradition, there are thirty-six-thousand to one-hundred-and-eight-thousand recognized extra-body meridian flows. Of this great number, differing traditions recognize that for the average human being, there are ten to twenty of these aura meridians that are powered with flowing energy from birth. The vast remainder are dormant. Some extraordinary humans who are psychic, geniuses of one sort or another, or very gifted from birth may be born with many more aura meridians lit up. But even in that group, well over ninety-nine percent of their aura meridians still remain dormant. Transformations of elemental fire energy are necessary to power all the potential dormant within us. Waking up the sleeping human energy system has been accomplished by spiritual adepts over the centuries practicing what is commonly known as the yoga of fire. In Tibetan Buddhism it is known as *tummo* or the practice of inner, psychic, or mystic heat.

Seven powerful and parallel energy wheels or chakras are stacked along the spine from the base to the crown that integrate different types of awareness. Different esoteric wisdom traditions describe them differently. Use your own awareness to explore what you find to be the nature of your own chakra system. Common to most traditions is that three central meridians transit the center of each chakra, the central balanced and linear channel and spiral twining yin and yang channels. Depending on what patterns are present at each chakra, a chakra will be more open or closed. Each chakra impinges on the three ascending vertical channels diminishing all their energy flows both up and down to some extent. The energy that flows through the central and side channels have three main influences. The first is karmic pressure that restricts free energy flow, whereas the design for enlightenment is for the side channels to flow very tranquilly and the central channel to be open fully. The second challenge is the flow in any of the meridians may be chaotic, sporadic, and uneven, which also diverts energy from returning to and entering the central channel. The last challenge is that all the chakras are powerful mass/energy/time transformers. In their normal functioning, they can and do shift suddenly to bring great changes, some changes ending life eras, or some catapulting us into entirely new sets of experiences. The more limiting the energy flow in closed chakras, the more forced and difficult is the karma that manifests interrupting our peaceful enjoyment of life.

The final energy structure to discuss here are *bindus* (Sanskrit) or *thigles* (Tibetan), which roughly mean essences, spheres, or orbs. In the body, we have hormones which are super concentrated essences compared, for instance, to blood. One drop of a hormone creates orders of change more than one drop of blood can. Similarly, there are concentrated, subtle essence orbs located throughout the physical and energy bodies. These energy orbs contain incredible potential, but like meridians outside the body, are largely inactive. When inner heat melts these bindus, they release their energy potential back into the interconnected human matrix of physical, energetic, and mental dimensions of living. The inner heat also untangles the tight intertwining of internal and external body energy flows. This relaxes the body, lightens and enlivens the flow of energy, and opens awareness, exponentially bringing ease, tranquility, and increasing freedom from constrictions.

Any yoga of mystic fire, including Spiral Dragon, has to accomplish a number of openings within our energy systems in order to catalyze a permanent and higher frequency shift. It has to tranquilize energy flow in all the channels and chakras. It has to open the channels gently and evenly so that qi energy moves more subtly toward and up the central channel. The mystic fire has to heat the whole body and energy flows to create more immediately available qi for health and living. The yogic fire must also increase intensity gradually enough so that it doesn't damage our physical and subtle body health. How much and how quickly each of us can harmoniously integrate the intensity of life fire energy varies. Next, yogic heat has to melt the bindus so that the very concentrated energy present in these essence orbs becomes available to add their synergy to power a quantum upward shift of consciousness. Spiral Dragon accomplishes each of these changes in a way that we can accommodate easily and naturally on our paths to awakening. Other systems accomplish the same goal, but they may steeply accelerate intensity of the yogic fire making that technique perilous for some practitioners.

The cosmos is a holistic organization from plancks to parsecs with every smaller manifestation mirroring every larger one at every scale. Spiral Dragon makes conscious use of this, beginning with the very first Relax exercise. When we relax body and mind, we focus attention somewhere—for instance, the forehead. If we succeed in letting go of stress at the forehead, but can't relax one hundred percent, we can still move on to the next focus area. This is because relaxing any focal area any amount relaxes the complete body-energy-mind complex contributing to exponential relaxation. The second application arises from the subsystems of TCM; eyes, ears, tongue, hands, and feet are a few holistic subsystems. Each reveals the whole health condition, and when activated, resonates with and heals whatever is dissonant. Working with any subsystem can increase your overall health to the highest level you have ever experienced. The one exception is the subsystem of the hands. Engaging the focus on hands in each exercise as Spiral Dragon allows you to exceed the highest level of health you have experienced so far in life. Finally, holistic progress does not unfold from an accumulation of gradual improvements. Rather, holistic accomplishment arises suddenly and spontaneously because it is already perfect in the uncreated mind. This is a completely different dynamic. The effort in Spiral Dragon is not in aggregating insights and skills over time, but in allowing your awareness to remain completely present in its original nature.

Spiral Dragon is an interplay of energies and awareness that is alive moment to moment. Practicing Spiral Dragon in an automatic, routine-like way of physical exercises doesn't create much transformation. Rather, being alive to self-arising and spontaneous movement accompanied by the influx of new insights and awareness creates positive and effortless transformation. Of course, it is easy to drift into automatic since that has become the hypnotic mindset of our era. Like meditative attention, when you notice you drift away from being present, just reset your posture and awareness and continue on with the experiment of Spiral Dragon. Spiral Dragon is an experiment in that it requires you to be a careful observer so you do notice encounters with the unexpected, whether that is about your self-perception, how others live their lives, the local environment, or even how the laws of physics seem to manifest in the moment. By looking into theses cracks in consciousness you discover and uncover yourself in the universe as it is.

Spiritual transformation systems can be closed or open depending upon the intention and approach of the practice. For instance, a self-development goal may be to balance and open your heart chakra to self-acceptance, self-love, or even unselfish love for others. To accomplish the goal, you work within the parameters of the heart organ, heart energies, and heart awareness all connecting at the heart chakra. It is an entire, interrelated method within the boundaries and measure of the closed, operational system of the chakra tree. Closed system transformation practices can be very effective in themselves in that they restore energy, health, balance, confidence, understanding, empathy, and connection with the greater cosmos. Spiral Dragon is an open system of energy and awareness which directly connects with the unlimited flows of the universe. The result leads to this exceptional claim that you will have to investigate for yourself: Spiral Dragon breaks the bounds of time. In closed inner transformation systems, practitioners draw renewed energies from their local environments, which replenish and expand their mind and energy fields. Spiral Dragon, however, operates beyond local time/space boundaries. By the second exercise, you can connect to anywhere in the universe at any time, past, present, or future. In times like now where there is serious depletion of the quality of air, water, and food, Spiral Dragon practice can enrich you with what your body and mind need to flourish. This happens through holistic resonance without conscious intention each time you practice. It also occurs with or without knowing the coordinates of your time/space connections.

The bounds of time and bounds of karma cocreate the limited worlds of our experiences. One definition of enlightenment is complete dissolution of karma in order to operate outside time limitations. Your very first practice of Spiral Dragon however will not completely dissolve the matrix of your perspectives, which are conditioned by the world you've created and live in. The long-term accumulation of your creations extending over lifetimes determines the karma you experience now. In fact, the root Sanskrit word for karma, *kri*, is related in meaning and even pronunciation to *create* in English. When you practice Spiral Dragon, you will experience easing of your karma so new insights can occur and new energies merge into your life field. As you continue to practice, though, you will begin to operate in a self-liberating dynamic and eventually learn how to apply this state of energy awareness to relieve pressure on yourself and others. Eventually you will be able to release long-standing knots that have blocked your health, abundance, and joy in living. The Spiral Dragon process of enlightenment arises moment to moment, but also creates a positive momentum of energy awareness that accelerates your continuous awakening to the unity of emptiness, clarity, wisdom, and bliss in the course of this very lifetime.

There are three major phases of transformation that you will be able to recognize as you practice Spiral Dragon. The first phase is immersion in and awareness of your energy structures like the acupuncture meridians. The state of these 21 channels and the 360 to 1000 recognized acupoints varies for everyone. The first phase includes being aware of how qi moves through your own chakras, meridians, and aura. This process is utterly unique, so each person will not have the same succession of experiences or even the same number of changes in awareness or energy that others will have. This means it is not helpful to make too detailed a comparison of your Spiral Dragon experiences with another practitioner. Certainly, you can discuss it, but you must realize that neither of you are a valid template of development for one another. You may have many similarities, but are not an exact path match for realizing enlightenment. In general, what you will experience is that your energy flow opens blocks in health, emotions, and understanding. Your qi becomes become more refined while the flow of qi becomes more tranquil. The result is that you begin to view and integrate your understanding of any event or phenomena from multiple angles at the same time which opens your awareness to function at higher levels.

The second phase of Spiral Dragon awareness encompasses the transformation of qi energy to light. As your energy body with its structures and flows continues to become ever more refined, you begin to experience the light of your own consciousness shining within you. It can shine from what appears to be outside what you consider to be you. You may experience lights of different colors, lights in the form of long or short cords or threads, light in the form of orbs, or diffuse or laser-like lights around you. In the light you will discover what may long have been in deep darkness or in shadow. Whether you practice in daylight or at night, you will be able to distinguish inner lights and their projection outward. When you practice under the external lights of the sun, moon, planets, stars, and nebulae, you will have different experiences of light. You may be able to see forms or displays of light waves and rays. What is projected from within into the outer sphere or from the outer world inward will seem to merge indistinguishably at times. The play of light and dark emerges and the archetypes of yin and yang stop being ideas and arise as experiences. The nature of this phase is that it moves from experience to experience until it concludes as each apparition is a temporary display.

In the third phase of Spiral Dragon transformation, you become aware that light carries information or knowledge with it. We now use the external technology of fiber optics as an innovation that allows information in audio, video, and data formats to be transmitted along thin, optical light fibers for great distances. In this phase of transformation, you become aware that light moving through internal, inherent technology of thousands of your own refined internal and external meridians indeed does carry, transmit, and receive information. As with all practices that convey advice, messages, or information, it is important for each practitioner to test and verify the validity of perceived information. In the *Yoga Sutras*, Patanjali presents *samyamna* as a similar result of completing the last three yogas of the eightfold Kriya yoga path. Samyamna is the ability to focus the mind on any topic to perceive and explore valid and true knowledge about that topic. This same yogic power is the result of the third phase of Spiral Dragon practice. Engaging this great wisdom beyond wisdom provides information both from within and from beyond the wheel of time. Buddhas and Bodhisattvas who have taken the vow to benefit all sentient beings unconditionally apply their access to omniscient scale knowledge to liberate all beings from the field of suffering and to lead them to the happiness of enlightened awareness.

During her thirteen-year retreat, Senton Dorje received the original Spiral Dragon yoga as twenty-two exercises which she taught to Master Quan. When I asked Master Quan to elaborate on the set of verbal instructions that he had received from Senton Dorje, he laughed saying that she had not provided any explanations of the practice beyond a physical demonstration and accompanying telepathic prompting. Over the course of practicing Spiral Dragon during the next twenty-one years he investigated the value and application of each exercise. Of these, he organized a main practice sequence of five exercises and concluding meditation. He also organized several other sequences for applying the energies of Spiral Dragon to develop the unique dharma of each practitioner.

As you will discover, Spiral Dragon is spontaneous and joyful self-discovery. When one of his students became confused about finding the right way to practice, he asked: "How do you know if you are making any progress with Spiral Dragon?" Master Quan answered: "If you are not becoming more intelligent, you are not practicing correctly!"

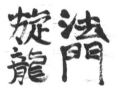

Fig. 2.1. Spiral Dragon Dharma Gate (Xuan² Long² Fa³ Men³).

3
Beginning Spiral Dragon
Relying upon Relaxation and Intuition

Start with Intention

Spiral Dragon can be practiced either as an accelerated way to manifest your life purpose skillfully, or it can be practiced as life purpose development together with realization of enlightenment. Before you begin each session, you should make your intention explicit. You don't have to recite a preset prayer or affirmation each time you begin. It is better on occasion to voice your own sincere thoughts and words as they arise in your heart and speak them directly to the heart of the universe. You can also address Senton Dorje and Master Quan in gratitude and for guidance. You can affirm your intention to benefit yourself and others with any prayers you recite daily. If you already practice a Buddhist tradition, you should add those aspirations, refuge, and Bodhisattva vows before you begin Spiral Dragon. You can intensify your intention by offering three sticks of incense at your altar, or in the area in which you will practice. The incense offering is an expression of gratitude for the teaching and an action to benefit all with the sublime fragrance that opens the hearts of all sentient beings and eases their afflictions.

34   Beginning Spiral Dragon

Fig. 3.1 Master Quan transmitting timeless connecting wisdom from in front of Kumbun Kalachakra Monastery in Xining.

In Figure 3.1 Master Quan is sending wisdom and qi. To receive the transmission, make the mirror mudras: place your left hand upward to receive, and place your open, right palm upward just below your navel. As you adopt this standing yoga posture, relax and be open. This posture also intensifies your intention to practice Spiral Dragon while making a direct connection with its gurus and source.

Exercises: Relax and Sky Dragon

The first two exercises, Relax and Sky Dragon, are the only two that must occur at the beginning of each Spiral Dragon session. These two exercises alone transform how you absorb and flow qi, light, and wisdom through your body, meridians, and consciousness. They also reset your connection to Earth and sky and the entire environment in flux in between. That relaxation is key for Spiral Dragon is clear in how it begins, and as you will discover, is essential to maintain in order to practice effectively. Relaxation obviously refers to the body, but it also includes the subtler levels of emotions, meridians, qi flow, and mind itself. On one level it seems odd that you have to practice relaxation, but we as humans are so wrought up within our own sensations and views, we often fail to see how far we are from relaxed moment to moment.

Exercise One
RELAX

1. Stand with your feet apart, toes pointing forward, and at the width of your shoulders. Place your arms at your side a few inches away from your torso to open up the flow through your arms and hands. Face your palms to the Earth as you do this practice. See Figure 3.2 on page 36. If you get too distracted initially by this, you can let your fingers point down, but within a week of beginning you should stand with palms facing down when possible. See Figure 3.3 on page 36. You will focus your attention on five parts of your body that have the greatest impact on relaxing you. Each of these areas (noted in the following steps) is a microsystem of the body. As you release tensions at the local spot, you are relaxing your whole body-mind complex.

2. Draw your attention to your forehead. Explore the sensations you are experiencing there. These sensations can be anything from discomfort to pain, depending on your condition. This condition changes from moment to moment so you only know what is happening when you are paying direct attention. Explore the sensation and feeling. One of three responses will happen. First, any discomfort you encounter will dissolve significantly. If that is the case move on to exploring another part of your forehead.

3. A second response is that as you become aware of the discomfort or pain you find, it doesn't seem to release much. However, if you continue to explore that discomfort, you will find that it will diminish on its own. It just needs more of your relaxed and directed attention to release. You do not have to try to release the discomfort because it happens automatically as you rest your attention there.

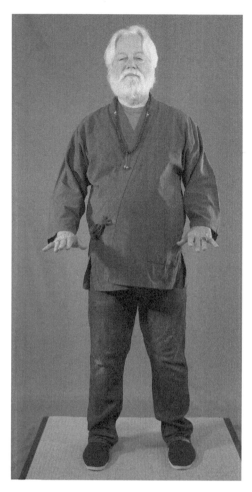

Fig. 3.2. Spiral Dragon initial Relax posture.
Photo by Kaleigh Brown.

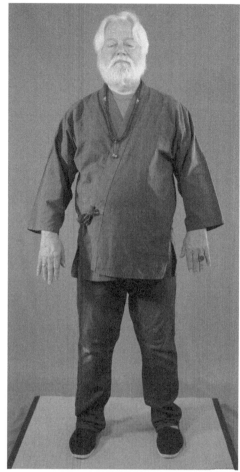

Fig. 3.3. Alternate hands position for Spiral Dragon Relax posture.
Photo by Kaleigh Brown.

4. The third response is that the pain you become aware of is more chronic in nature, and you may be aware of it often because it draws your attention. You will counter by more deeply exploring what you find. You will see how it connects in your body, how it triggers, and how it diminishes. Take your time to explore this. Five minutes is not too much to do this exploration unless you feel caught in the emotion of frustration. The discomfort will

decrease by some amount, but it may not be more than half. If that case, chant the sound **HA** under your breath to release the remainder of the discomfort. Note what happened, then move on. The forehead focus of Relax releases physical knots of tension.

5. Next focus on your eyebrows and the point between your eyebrows. Allow your attention to explore this area fully. Any of the three responses may occur which are a sudden release of discomfort, a slower and partial release, or the need to chant the silent **HA** to release the more difficult knots of tension you find. This part of Relax releases being bothered by the parade of thoughts.

6. Next focus on the backs of your knees, which you can do directly or indirectly, whichever you find easier as you practice. Draw your attention directly to the backs of your knees and feel any tension held there. Again, you can have one of the three responses of release; if you first settle your attention on your knees and they release, there is no need to do anything else but move on. You can try the indirect method by noting the amount of energy above your knee versus below it. If they are about the same level, the knee joint is open so flow can happen. If you find a difference, you can allow your knee to open by focusing your attention there. When both above and below the knee are nearly equal, you can move on. You can also chant a silent **HA** if you have difficulty letting go.

7. Next, focus on the soles of your feet. There is just one acupuncture point located there, number one on the Kidney channel (KI). It is called *yong³quan²* meaning *gushing spring*. Like the knees, you can relax the soles of the feet directly or indirectly. For directly, place your attention on the soles of your feet and explore what tension you encounter. Again, there are three possible responses to allowing release of tension. If you use the indirect method, the name of the acupuncture point, gushing spring, is more relevant. Like the knees you will look above the soles and below the soles of the feet. If you feel that energy flows faintly through your feet into the Earth or is impaired in gushing upward from the Earth through the soles of your feet, you need to allow your feet to relax and open more. You want to allow the free flow of qi through your soles whether the flow you experience is up or down.

8. The next focus point arises spontaneously. Regard your body as a whole and feel what part is still in discomfort. Your body will grab your attention, so just allow that attention to settle where it is drawn and to explore what you find. Again, your exploration may quickly resolve the discomfort of pain, or it make take a bit more effort. This last focus of relaxation is open ended as you may have ten areas of your body calling for your attention. Don't attempt to resolve every pain, just go for the top three to five. At the end of relaxation, whether or not you have used it before, chant **HA** silently and think as you do so that you release the entirety of discomfort in your body, emotions, and thoughts. Take a moment to feel the difference.

Performing Sky Dragon

The Sky Dragon exercise increases our resonance with the spiral dynamic and establishes Spiral Dragon as an open system practice. You can think of it as the direct connector between orders of magnitude in the universe from subatomic to super galactic. It makes it easy to navigate between scales of magnitude in the holistic universe where each scale is a perfect reflection of the ones above and below. This exercise also opens doors across space-time limitations. For these reasons, it is important to practice Sky Dragon correctly. If it's not activated, then your practice moves within the slow bounds of local space, time, and karma. When executed properly, you are practicing in an open, accelerated, and responsive universe. That said, it is easy to practice Sky Dragon correctly and to confirm to yourself that you are operating within that transformational state.

Sky Dragon has two parts. The first is an extension of Relax, but applied to the spine in order to relax more deeply to open the energy meridians, the central channel, and chakras. The second part involves a stretch of the spine. Although there are precise physical components to each exercise and meditation, remember that Spiral Dragon is not a set of physical exercises, but primarily an integrated continuum of energy exercises executed from a single point of meditative presence.

Each practitioner has different potentials and experiences. Some may feel this transformation the very first time they practice, while almost everyone will experience clear signs of transformation within the first week of practice. Over the course of your life, you will enter this state and drift away later until your Spiral Dragon practice establishes that dynamic as constant.

Exercise Two

SKY DRAGON

1. Continue to stand now in a more relaxed posture with feet at the width of your shoulders, with arms slightly away from your sides and palms facing earthward. Direct your attention to the center of your spine beginning at the base, then move upward as you relax and release tension from within the column of each vertebra. Relaxing the whole spine is important in being able to stretch and open the spine physically, and open the central channel energetically.

2. Start at the base, the coccyx, which has three to five fused rudimentary vertebrae. This is the chakra that allows kundalini energy to rise upward, but it is doubly protected by two internal gates. Also protected with two internal gates are the heart and third-eye chakras. All three of these may require extra attention to invoke the relaxed state and to ease the flow of qi through them. As you examine your spine from the inside, you may be able to experience each vertebra individually, or you may experience several vertebrae as a unit of perception. Work with what you perceive at the moment. Over time your ability to focus on more precise areas of your body will increase easily and naturally with practice.

3. As you place your attention on each vertebra, feel any tension present there. With each specific focus, there are three possible responses, exactly as in the Relax exercise, that reflect the condition of your body and energy at that moment and location. The first possibility is that as you discover the tension, very quickly the tension melts under the gaze of your mind.

Secondly, the tension might persist as you examine it, but eventually, it substantially releases. Finally, you may examine a vertebra for a longer period yet not experience significant release. That is when you chant **HA** silently to fully release whatever hasn't been released. Then you move on and up.

4. Move up your spine methodically and take your time. As you first begin to practice Spiral Dragon, you might spend a half hour just on the first two exercises. Even later, as a more seasoned practitioner, you might devote a longer effort to relaxing your spine, especially if you've stressed it by exercise, long car drives, or injury. Each practice time is unique. Be present moment to moment and be responsive to your condition as you find it.

Fig. 3.4. Sky Dragon posture.
Photo by Kaleigh Brown.

5. When you have relaxed the full length of the spine you are ready to stretch. Rather than simply bending your head backward instead move your head up and then bend it back a bit. Move your head upward then backward in steps which will uplift your entire spinal column in ease. Keep stretching up and back for a count of twenty-one. Don't force this stretch so that it pinches or causes discomfort in your neck. Rather, let it occur with ease and openness. See Figure 3.4 above. If you feel tension in your neck as you stretch upward, the tension is arising from somewhere along your spine and not necessarily from stiffness in your neck. At the end of counting twenty-one, bring your head forward slowly and also raise it up toward the sky in reverse order of the backward stretch. Relax your body and energy and take note of your condition.
6. The stretch and immediate relaxation after Sky Dragon is essential to accelerating your connection and facility to energy and awareness. Take the time to do several repetitions of both parts of this exercise until you feel some change. Each person will perceive sensations arising differently. A common response is that you feel swaying in the spine. It may be similar to the sensation of standing on a dock of a small lake, then noticing the water swells move up and down through your body. Or it may be more intense. Remember, everyone will not have the same experience of Spiral Dragon in the same sequence or intensity. Experiencing the unexpected, accepting and exploring it, is the inner path of Spiral Dragon.

Once you have experienced the deep relaxation and opening of the Relax and Sky Dragon exercises, you can begin to apply them in your daily life activities immediately. First is working with the experience of physical flexibility. We assume that flexibility results because we have done muscle stretching exercises that make our bodies more limber. From the Spiral Dragon experience, and the experience of other systems of energy exercise, our root flexibility derives from the condition of our energy flow. To test the truth of this, try an experiment. Do a stretch such as touching your toes. Then do the Relax and Sky Dragon exercises, but don't do any physical stretch before touching your toes again. You can even bend your head backward in a moving Sky Dragon motion as you bend to touch your toes. Compare your flexibility after the physical versus the energy stretch. As you test this with many stretches where you feel physically stiff, you will see that flexibility is primarily a quality of your energy flow, whereas your muscles, ligaments, and body mass respond, but are secondary.

Second, if you are a meditator, you can do your regular meditation practice right after these initial exercises. If you are a healer, artist, musician, writer, teacher, chef, or athlete, engage your usual skills and notice if there is a difference in the quality or result of the discipline you are good at. There is no limit to how you can experiment. What you are doing is comparing the results of working your skills normally and then again compared after the first two Spiral Dragon exercises. In my experience what happens is you may or may not improve your performance on the spot, but you do get many creative insights about how to improve your results going forward. If I am brushing *kanji** right after these two exercises, I can see the difference immediately and so can others. Usually, these two exercises alone provide the inspiration that develops a big jump forward in your knowledge and skills.

What happens during the first two Spiral Dragon exercises is that you switch your experience field from being closed and limited to open and cosmic. An example is a mind-boggling experiment that you can do if you haven't done it already. Start with a strip of paper and draw a line on one side. When you join the ends of the strip with a piece of tape it makes a loop with two surfaces, an inner one and an outer one. Remove the tape, then twist the paper strip a half turn and re-tape it. You will notice that the line you drew only goes halfway around the surfaces. The surprise comes when you trace your finger on the surface and discover there is now only one continuous surface that has no inside nor outside. There is no end and no beginning. In fact, the paper strip that you made will actually resemble a three-dimensional symbol of the

---

*Brushing kanji (often called *Shodo* in Japanese) is the practice of writing Chinese or Japanese characters using a calligraphy brush and ink. The East Asian art of calligraphy expresses a fusion of linguistic, artistic, and energetic threads to create greater meaning and impact.

Fig. 3.5. A mobius strip resembles the infinity symbol. Originally there are two separate surfaces. The half-twist of the strip, however, creates a single, continuous surface with no inside nor outside, but with a never-ending flow instead.
Adobe license.

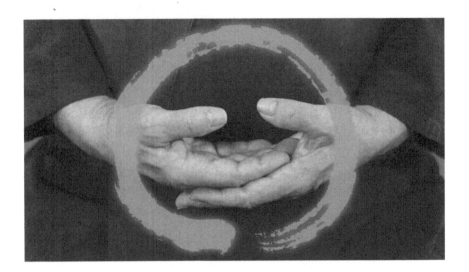

Fig. 3.6. Infinity view of Spiral Dragon meditation mudra with enso.
Composite artwork by Kaleigh Brown.

infinity sign. See Figure 3.5 above illustrating a mobius strip which is what your half-turn twisted paper strip has now become.

I encountered a three-dimensional mobius strip track at the Museum of Science and Industry in Chicago when I was in elementary school. It had a little car that drove in one direction and never stopped as it made infinite circuits. Why I emphasize this example is because it is aptly analogous to what Sky Dragon accomplishes in Spiral Dragon. The extremely simple change is opening your energy in the way described in the exercise. It is just like the half twist of a paper strip because it transforms limited recurring circuits into one infinite flow. Sky Dragon transforms dualistic perception into infinite and holistic experience with unexpected ease and profound results. This transformation is reflected symbolically in the Spiral Dragon meditation mudra with an *enso** superimposed as shown in Figure 3.6 on page 43.

There is an aspect of Spiral Dragon that is objectively measurable. Before introductory Spiral Dragon training, Master Quan often used an electroacupuncture test developed by Reinhard Voll, MD (1909–1989) to determine the electrical conductivity of a few key acupuncture points.[1] Dr. Voll's basic method was developed with a companion software program by many manufacturers and Master Quan used a proprietary brand current in the early 1990s. The test determined a percentage of how open the body is to electromagnetic flow, which is also a measure of how robust a person's life force and health are. Even if the baseline tests were in the seventy percent range beforehand, the results at the end of seminar improved significantly to the mid to high nineties for many students. Master Quan had a keen interest in exploring Spiral Dragon as both an outer and inner science.

**Enso* (Japanese for *circle*)—an almost complete circle drawn in one continuous brushstroke is a demonstration of Zen mind of wisdom beyond wisdom. It connects the viewer with the whole universe and is perfection in direct simplicity. Enso is a gate to infinite experience.

4
Moving and Integrating Energy
Hands, Breath, and Thought

Connecting directly through the central spinal channel to the primary energies of the universe is the most important step of Spiral Dragon. Once that connection is made, we want to allow that energy to circulate more freely through the body and aura in an increasingly relaxed and open flow. The next three exercises gently open a greater flow through the main and peripheral energy channels both in the plane of the body and in the near space outside the body. Engaging in these three exercises also creates greater awareness and skill in absorbing and expelling, and in moving and stilling, these energies. These exercises are the practical bridge for applying Spiral Dragon to improving life to benefit yourself and others.

Performing Spiral Dragon Hands

This exercise generates great energy, dynamic tension, and heat that begins in the hands and arms and moves inward to the torso. It is a way to ignite the energy system so you can integrate increasing intensity without causing yourself extreme reactions. Nonetheless, Spiral Dragon is a powerful yoga of fire. By maintaining a state of relaxation while moving and feeling energies enter, circulate, and exit your body and energy field, you will remain in the center of the eye of transformation. Because this is an energy exercise, it is organized in cycles of twenty-one repetitions. As mentioned previously, this number corresponds to the twenty-one channels that form human acupuncture energy flows, composed of two central vertical meridians, twelve vertical jing meridians and seven horizontal luo meridians. Twenty-one repetitions create a basic energy measure or cycle which itself is then repeated three, seven, fourteen, or twenty-one times. Because Spiral Dragon is also the play of consciousness, perform each of the repetitions from a relaxed, centered, and aware state of mind.

Exercise Three

SPIRAL DRAGON HANDS

1. Like the previous exercises, stand with your feet apart in line with your shoulders, and hold your hands at your sides palms facing the Earth. See Figure 3.2 in the previous chapter (page 36).
2. Re-examine your body to see if you continue to experience the overall relaxed and open state that you experienced at the conclusion of both the Relax and Sky Dragon exercises.
3. If you find that you're feeling tense or in discomfort, then go through the Relax and Sky Dragon exercises again. When you re-perform these exercises, it will become easier and quicker each time you do so in the same session. If you're still relaxed and connected to the sky energies, then move to the next step.
4. While keeping your arms extended at a forty-five degree angle to the Earth, rotate your palms inward to the center while keeping your arms relatively straight. See Figure 4.1 below. Touch your two middle fingers together, relax, and ease your palms outward a few inches. The first time you do this, hold this posture while remaining relaxed for a count of twenty-one. After this, move your palms facing down by your sides at the

level of your navel. This exercise, the most intense of the series, generates heat and intensity which will become more comfortable to experience over time.

5. Relax again before you do a second or third repetition of this exercise. As you progress, you will be able to maintain the relaxed state even during many repetitions. What is important is to recognize when you begin doing more muscular or physical exercise instead of energy exercise with ease.

Fig. 4.1. Spiral Dragon Hands, initial rotated hands posture.
Photo by Kaleigh Brown.

Fig. 4.2. Spiral Dragon Hands, rotated pulsing posture.
Photo by Kaleigh Brown.

6. After you do a few sessions with the static rotation of your hands, you can add dynamic energy pulsing. Rotate your palms inward, but place your arms at a forty-five degree angle, so you can pulse energy into the Earth. This pulsing, push, and release expels your energy into the Earth. See Figure 4.2 above. A common mistake is making a large pushing and retracting motion with hands and arms. When moving energy and not muscles, you only need to pulse a few centimeters. Someone observing your practice will notice only slight movements on your part.

7. Feel the pulse arise from your navel, move up your spine to the shoulders, then branch through each arm. Feel the pulse move out of your body through the center of your palms and into the Earth to a depth of three meters. If you were to locate this point at the center of either palm by acupuncture anatomy, it is *lao^{2}gong^1*, the eighth point on the Pericardium channel (PC8). Another way to locate this point is by bending your second and third fingers to touch the center of your palm, noting the point between your bent fingers. Using this method, you will notice that the change in flexibility of your fingers will reveal a slightly different location each time you check. The energy centers of the palms are not fixed, but are in fluid motion. You may also want to notice how the center area lines of your palms shift as you engage Spiral Dragon.

8. As you practice this exercise more, increase your sense of pulsing and projecting energy eventually to a depth of twenty-six kilometers. Master Quan often repeated the instruction to project your qi to a depth of twenty-six kilometers or almost sixteen miles. This creates a deep connection with the Earth that has many applications you can discover with continuing experience.

9. With each energy pulse, you project a rough energy into the Earth. As you release and relax, a more refined qi filtered through the Earth immediately reenters your body and aura. Some practitioners may worry they might lose their energy doing this exercise, however, when you pulse your energy outwardly, it remains connected with you. Because of this, no matter how far you pulse your energy out, it will return completely and immediately, but also in a clearer and purer state. You do not have to visualize refining your qi because it occurs naturally and of itself.

Moving and Integrating Energy   49

An important and practical consideration arises here about how far you need to rotate your hands inward together, and how much of an elbow bend you can have for this exercise to work. Over time by practicing Spiral Dragon, your energy and then your body will become more flexible so that you automatically practice more effectively. The challenge is assuring that your practice works well from the beginning. There is a test you can perform to check yourself. The key point is that as you rotate your arms and hands inwardly, you open an energetic gate in your shoulders allowing energy from arms and torso to merge. This gate has to be open for energy to flow freely. The test is to rotate one of your arms inwardly while placing the fingers of your opposite hand on the shoulder joint you are rotating. See Figure 4.3 below.

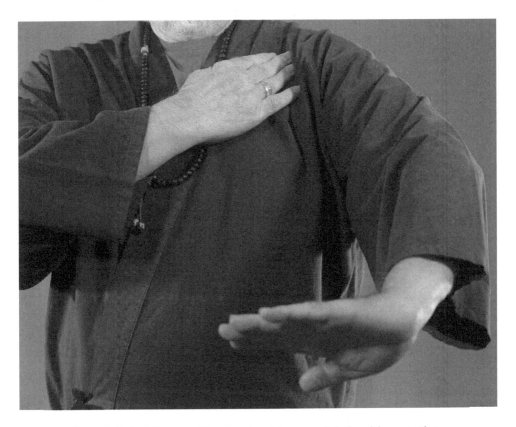

Fig. 4.3. Spiral Dragon Hands, checking crucial shoulder rotation.
Photo by Kaleigh Brown.

1. Keep your arms as straight and unbent as is comfortable to start. Rotate in and out a few times and to feel the bones and muscles of the shoulder gate open and close.
2. Next, experiment by bending your arm a little bit more each time as you rotate the hand inward then outward. The fingers on your shoulder should feel when the gate opens and closes. You will discover that after a certain arm-bending point, you no longer feel the muscles and bones shift and open. It's pointless to do this exercise when the gate is in a closed position because there will be minimal to negligible qi circulation.

Performing Spiral Dragon Fingers

The next two exercises, Spiral Dragon Fingers and Spiral Dragon Palms, move qi within and through the body and aura. Both of these have very practical applications, most immediately for health. The Spiral Dragon Fingers exercise circulates more yang energy which benefits the yin parts of your body. In this case the front of your body, especially your internal organs, are stimulated to a greater degree. If you have difficulties or discomfort with the functioning of any of your organ systems, for example digestion, then practice this exercise more consciously for a longer time and it will lessen your body's immediate discomfort and dysfunction. When you practice, you don't have to target specifically your digestive system, you just have to practice with overall attention, watching what is happening. Spiral Dragon energies seem to possess an adaptive intelligence to harmonize whatever is most out of balance. In each moment, simply place your attention where you experience physical difficulty, and in a holistic manner, Spiral Dragon energies will begin adjusting and healing you.

You can immediately move in sequence from one exercise to the next if you are relaxed. If you are not relaxed, go back to repeat the Relax and Sky Dragon exercises which establish underlying and dynamic relaxation that connects you intimately to the cosmos. Or, you may just need to let go of tension in your arms, hands, and body from the last exercise to reestablish that dynamic connection. This exercise and the next one each have an alternate version; the first method is for those just starting out, and the second is for experienced practitioners. The second version is the one you will use most usually. From the very position of the last exercise with your arms extended at a forty-five-degree angle to the Earth and with palms rotated inward and facing forward, move your palms so that they face toward your navel chakra. You don't need to move much, except to adjust your posture more precisely. Check that you are relaxed, then proceed.

Exercise Four
SPIRAL DRAGON FINGERS

1. Bring your hands together and touch your middle fingers, then slowly draw them apart a few inches. See Figures 4.4 and 4.5 on page 52. This is a good moment to check that your hands are indeed at the same level as your navel.
2. Slowly move your hands just a few centimeters toward one another, which is sufficient to feel a magnetic field resisting your fingertips and fingers. Next, release the movement and feeling of resistance. Your hands will automatically repel from one another the few centimeters you had just pushed. Do this push/release exercise twenty-one times as one set and repeat in sets of three, seven, fourteen, or twenty-one.
3. Next, you pull your hands slowly and slightly apart, the opposite of what you just did. Again, you will feel a resistance to pulling. When you let go of pulling, your hands will recoil a few centimeters back to the position from which you began. Again, do this pull/release exercise twenty-one times as one set and repeat sets of three, seven, fourteen, or twenty-one times. After a week or two of practicing the push and pull method separately, you can move to the next step. The main point is for you to be able to clearly feel the magnetic field of both attraction and resistance in your hands and fingers. Playing back and forth with this universal magnetic field accelerates qi circulation and saturates your body and aura in the galactic and intergalactic medium that connects everything.

Fig. 4.4. Spiral Dragon Fingers initial position.
Photo by Kaleigh Brown.

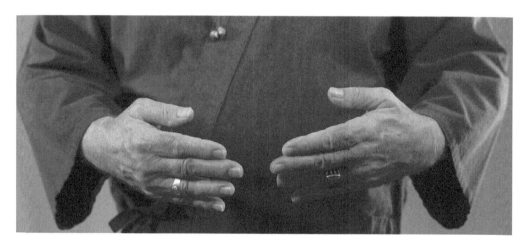

Fig. 4.5. Spiral Dragon Fingers, push-pull next position.
Photo by Kaleigh Brown.

4. You are now going to combine push and pull into one cycle. When you push your fingers together and experience the magnetic resistance, let go. As your fingers move apart, pull slightly apart at the same time. It won't take very long for you to combine push/release then pull/release into a continuous motion. In the beginning, speed is your enemy because it will turn this movement into a muscle exercise. Take your time so you can experience the magnetic flow of qi shifting in your hands, so eventually

you will be able to track that flow through your whole body. The cycle consists of push/release followed by pull/release, which you will repeat twenty-one times as one set, then repeat sets of three, seven, fourteen, or twenty-one times as before.

The key point for this and the next exercise is to experience and play with the magnetic field. In Chinese language, you might ask: Do you play taiji?* Similarly in English we ask: Do you play music? Both inquiries could have used the word *practice* which suggests a certain amount of forced discipline, but both use the word *play* instead. This is exactly how you should approach all of Spiral Dragon, as elaborate and creative play. It is about wondrous discovery moment to moment.

Performing Spiral Dragon Palms

As before, you can immediately move from the previous exercise to Spiral Dragon Palms if you are operating from a state of dynamic relaxation. If you scan yourself and find that tension has replaced relaxation, then you need to repeat the Relax and Sky Dragon exercises to reestablish your energetic harmony with the universe. Over many sessions of Spiral Dragon, you will become more and more skilled in assessing your physical, emotional, and mental degree of distress and being able to release the amount of tension you hold. Spiral Dragon Palms exercise circulates more yin energy and benefits the yang parts of your body. Your entire back is yang in nature so if you have back aches, the Spiral Dragon Palms exercise will move more healing energy through that part of your body, especially your lower back. If you have back pain or tension, then you can adjust your Spiral Dragon session to include more of this exercise to create immediate as well as long-term benefit.

**Taiji* and tai chi or tai chi chuan refer to the same movement art. The spellings reflect the two popular spelling conventions, the older Wade-Giles and newer Pinyin, to show Chinese Mandarin pronunciation in Roman letters. In this book, I have used the Pinyin system.

Exercise Five

SPIRAL DRAGON PALMS

1. From your last posture with fingers almost touching one another and hands held at the level of your navel, simply move your palms outward so they now face one another. Make the minimum movement necessary. See Figure 4.6 below.

2. Exactly as in the last exercise there is a beginner learning method and a usual practice method for pushing and pulling. The beginner method separates the exercise into two steps, whereas the usual practice method is to combine pushing and pulling into a continuous movement cycle.

3. For the initial week or two of learning, hold your palms six inches apart. Start by pushing your palms toward one another a few centimeters, but as you feel resistance from the magnetic quality of space, release, allowing your hands to recoil slightly farther apart. See Figure 4.7 below. Feeling the magnetic quality of the space around you is much easier playing palm to palm than finger to finger. Repeat this twenty-one times as a set, then repeat that set three, seven, fourteen, or twenty-one times.

4. Now, do the separate complementary motion of pulling your palms away from each other a few centimeters. This time you will feel the magnetic resistance more on the backs of your hands. When you do, let go of your effort and allow your hands to recoil back toward one another. Repeat this twenty-one times as a set, then repeat that set three, seven, fourteen, or twenty-one times.

5. After you experience Spiral Dragon for a week or two, experiment with combining the push/release and pull/release into a continuous movement. As before with Spiral Dragon Fingers, this creates a cycle to repeat twenty-one times as a set. Repeat the continuous motion set of Spiral Dragon palms three, seven, fourteen, or twenty-one times.

If you have trouble feeling the magnetic nature of qi play in either of the above two exercises, make three subtle adjustments. Relax. Move your

Moving and Integrating Energy   55

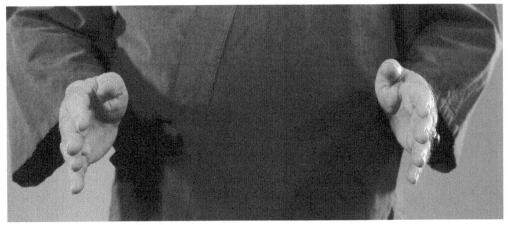

Fig. 4.6. Spiral Dragon Palms, initial posture.
Photo by Kaleigh Brown.

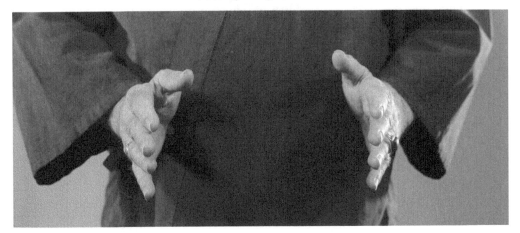

Fig. 4.7. Spiral Dragon Palms, push-pull next position.
Photo by Kaleigh Brown.

hands back in direct alignment at the level of your navel. Push and pull more slowly. These three easy adjustments will immediately increase the magnetic sense of play you feel.

Performing Spiral Dragon Meditation

It is important to include meditation at the end of actively moving energy through your body and aura. Do Spiral Dragon Meditation for at least ten minutes to conclude each session, which will more subtly integrate the energy and awareness you have just accelerated. The secret of this meditation, similar to Zen, is that the standing energy practice you have already done is itself a moving meditation. You will discover that it has already dissolved many energy knots and mental distractions that normally perturb your body and mind during meditation. In other words, it is many times easier to settle into sitting meditative mind after standing Spiral Dragon energy play and practice. Your mind is already more alert and relaxed as you change physical positions. Later, you can extend Spiral Dragon Meditation for forty minutes or longer at the end of the other exercises.

There are many variations of cross-legged, seated meditative postures you can strike to establish presence of body and mind as you sit at Earth level. Although you can sit cross-legged on the ground, the preferred posture for Spiral Dragon Meditation is seated on a simple chair that will allow you to sit upright on the front third of the chair seat. This reflects the imagery of the next Buddha to come, Maitreya, who is shown seated on a throne, feet touching the Earth. Some tantric gurus are also shown in sacred art sitting on a chair illustrating this intentional posture. As with all meditations there are synergistic ways to hold your body, breathe, and be present and aware. Spiral Dragon Meditation posture addresses how to place your spine, legs and feet, arms and hands, tongue and gaze, which is described below in steps. This creates the container of the outer form. Since Spiral Dragon is based upon open and spontaneous interplay of mind, feeling, and movement, feel your breath at the navel, but allow it to be free to settle into and cycle through any arising patterns as long as you exert no conscious control. Similarly, tether your attention to your navel and breath, then be wholly present without artifice, making no attempt to control the arising or disappearance of thoughts. After you arrange your body, breath, and mind, make subtle adjustments when you find that your body moves out of posture or when your mind wanders. The meditation instructions are divided in three sections below: body posture, breath and breathing, and mind and thoughts.

Meditation

BODY POSTURE

1. Sit upright in a chair on the front third of the chair seat making sure that your spine is straight. You need to straighten your spine and not lean forward nor backward.
2. Place your feet on the floor in front of you, crossing your right ankle over your left.
3. Place your hands into the meditation mudra by putting your right palm on top of your left palm. Use your index fingers to make a precise connection by placing the right knuckle over the left so the lines of both joints line up. Then hold your cupped palms upward touching just below your navel. Make sure your thumbs point toward each other but do not touch. Place your arms in an oval so that you continue to allow energy to circulate. If your arms collapse against your sides, it will close your shoulder gates diminishing or stopping circulation of qi. This posture is shown in Figure 4.8 on page 58.
4. As you meditate let your tongue rest on your lower palate. Some meditations, like zazen, prescribe your tongue to touch the roof of your mouth. Spiral Dragon has a reason. Because you intentionally leave a gap both at the thumbs and tongue, it creates the necessity for the energy flow to arc across at both places. This adds a quality to the qi flow that you can investigate for yourself. See Figure 4.9 on page 58.
5. Hold your head upright, eyes forward, and nose in line with your navel and central spinal axis.

As to your eyes, there are four possible positions you are free to explore. With your eyes closed, gaze into the light that shines through the dark interior. Next, with eyes open slightly, gaze downward at a forty-five-degree angle looking at nothing in particular in that view, but sensing everything. These two are especially recommended until you establish a stable meditation. The third eye position is to gaze open-eyed directly ahead. In most environments, this

Fig. 4.8. Spiral Dragon Meditation in a chair.
Photo by Kaleigh Brown.

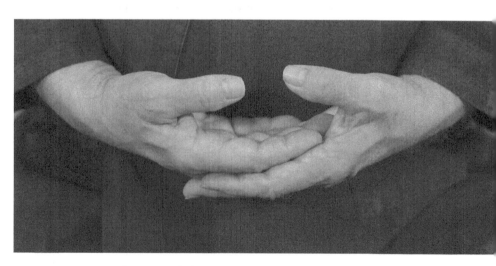

Fig. 4.9. Spiral Dragon Meditation hand mudra.
Photo by Kaleigh Brown.

is where the majority of visual clutter exists, which unless your meditation is extremely stable is the least recommended gaze to use. Finally, with head facing forward and eyes open, cast your gaze upward at a forty-five-degree angle. Do not look directly into the sun, but rather look into clear azure portion of the sky. At night, look into an area of clear space where stars are shining. If you find a gaze distracting, don't continue using it in this session; if you find one of the gazes to be more stabilizing, use that.

MEDITATIVE BREATH AND BREATHING

1. Take a few initial deep breaths after you settle your body into the optimal posture. Feel the breath arise from your navel.
2. Let your breathing regulate itself. During the course of meditation, it may shift in speed, depth, sound resonance, and subtlety. Let it. Breathe through your nose or mouth and allow the arising breath pattern to adjust itself naturally.
3. In general, and over the long run, your breath will become slower and more subtle of itself. Don't impose that intention in the short run.

MEDITATIVE MIND AND THOUGHTS

1. Once your body and breathing settle, place attention at the area directly behind your navel at the center of your spine. This is the home focus of your meditation that you will return to whenever you notice that you have become distracted by sensations or thoughts. Establishing, re-establishing, and maintaining this connection is the method.
2. Earlier, you did a push-pull exercise with your fingers and then with your palms, so you know how to recognize the magnetic feeling and the resistance it creates. Next, do a few rounds of push-pull between the tip of your nose and the area directly behind your navel. This makes some people slightly nauseous, but it is a way to verify that these two areas are connected by attention and by energy. When the two are connected, you will feel an energy at both locations.
3. Spiral Dragon is a one-pointed approach. Once you feel an energy sensation in one or both locations, it is palpable evidence that the two are

connected. Whichever place, nose or navel, has the greatest sensation is where you should tether and maintain your attention.

4. When thoughts arise, let them pass as you remain undistracted. If, however, a thought, emotion, or body sensation distracts your steady attention, then you have to readjust. Distractions, even thinking, cut lines of connecting energy between body and mind. This has far-reaching implications for health. Once again, use the nose and navel push-pull technique to re-establish mental and energetic connected presence.

5. Sometimes you may become distracted because you slipped out of the optimum posture. When that happens check and adjust your body. Appreciate in that moment, and in greater depth later in post-meditation moments, how intimately structured yet relaxed body posture affects sensation, breathing, and attention. You only need to examine your posture when distraction arises.

6. Over a long-term period of Spiral Dragon meditative experiences, you will begin to recognize interruptions to energy flow directly. Always patiently and calmly reconnect so that you maintain body, energy, and mind connection. Many positive health improvements, insights, and calm intensity arise of themselves without you ever needing to make conscious intentions or arrangements. This is the effort of no effort.

Spiral Dragon play and meditation are arts of living. As such, they each have great breadth and depth as well as infinite applications to all your possible interests. At this point, I have presented the purpose and history of Spiral Dragon plus the basics of how to practice. Within these topics I have presented the most common concerns about how to do Spiral Dragon well. In the next few chapters, I will explore more details of the practice and play, but at this moment you now have all the essential details to enter Spiral Dragon fully. It will take you a number of sessions before you remember and perform the details described so far. When you are ready for both more of the finer and more of the galactic implications of Spiral Dragon, read on. It will make more sense that way.

5
Restoring Your Health and Energy
Recalling, Recharging, and Rebalancing Qi Energy

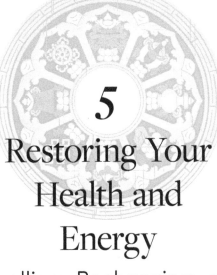

Practicing Spiral Dragon When Ill

Let us consider how to deal with obstacles to Spiral Dragon practice. These range from feeling a bit lazy and unmotivated to feeling quite ill. If you have an emergency illness, you should of course seek emergency medical help. If you are recovering from a very severe, exhaustive illness, there are adaptations of Spiral Dragon you can apply to accelerate your healing. Those we will consider later. To start, Master Quan discovered a mantra that is useful when you are feeling ill. It works especially quickly for any mild discomfort or illness you experience. If that is your condition before Spiral Dragon, you can restore your sense of wellness by chanting **AUM SHA HUM ZHN CHIN OM SO HA** twenty-one or one-hundred eight times.

Please refer to Appendix 1 for a compilation of mantras and pronunciation guide (page 139).*

The next case is when you are feeling a cold or flu, and aren't able to stand and practice. Ironically, you may feel you don't have the energy for that. The following practice is not part of the main sequence of Spiral Dragon. You can use it anytime you want, however, in order to begin the sequence, to strengthen your qi, or use to experiment. If you're not feeling able to stand for the whole practice, you may combine sitting and standing postures as you need as described below.

First, bear in mind the *adaptogenic* quality of Spiral Dragon when you seek to heal yourself or others. That Spiral Dragon is adaptogenic means it self-selectively acts on what most needs balancing. You already may have encountered adaptogenic actions of some herbs like ginseng or essential oils and marveled at how they stimulated whatever needed to be healed. It seems as if a natural intelligence is at play. Spiral Dragon energies combined with your own conscious awareness exercise a palpable, inseparable intelligence that can unravel the exact sequential causes for your disease if you allow it. If you think you have identified what is the cause of your own illness and how it unfolded, you may be correct or not. If you insistently direct energy to what you think is the key physiological cause and it is not, you may slow your healing down. Healing methods based on the path of liberation exhibit a natural, intelligent, holistic process that continuously restores life force and health balance. When you come to experience this type of healing, you can rely on it more and more, and allow it to unfold naturally.

Second, recognize that the imbalances that cause disease are the

---

*Mantras are sound vibrations that change when moving through the complex medium of your body, emotions, energy, and awareness. They attune to your presence, and in turn, you may tune them to resonate more harmonically. Any spelling of a mantra is an approximation that points to how to generate a sound, but requires each of us to fine-tune it. The **AUM** mantra represents three sounds blended together. The continuous blending may vary in elongation depending on the whole mantra in which it appears, and on your own condition when you chant.

same imbalances of karma that cloud your own enlightenment. Viewed this way, enlightenment is the ultimate cure for all diseases that disturb heart and mind. Healing is really a fundamental and necessary practice on the path of enlightenment. The point is do not skip self-healing because you think you don't have time. Some degree of healing is important for you to be able to relax and dynamically engage cosmic energies through Spiral Dragon. If chanting **AUM SHA HUM ZHN CHIN OM SO HA** has not helped much, then try doing the next exercise to expel imbalanced qi and improve your health.

Expelling Imbalanced Qi

Performing this exercise usefully relies on your experience learning all the previous Spiral Dragon exercises. Engaging this exercise especially allows you to alternate sitting and standing postures as you practice. As described in chapter three, before you begin practice, have a chair close behind you so that you can sit down right away if you feel dizziness or nausea arise. This is more important here, especially since you are starting the practice already feeling ill. I will describe the exercise as done from a standing posture, but if you can't, it is better to sit and practice.

Exercise

EXPELLING IMBALANCED QI

1. Stand with both feet at shoulders' length apart, arms at your sides with palms facing the Earth.
2. Perform the Relax and Sky Dragon exercises as described in chapter three if you are able. If you are unable to do them, then move ahead, but first take three deep breaths making the **HA** sound silently with each exhalation.
3. Perform the next four steps in one coordinated movement together even

64   Restoring Your Health and Energy

Fig. 5.1. Expelling Imbalanced Qi, initial posture balancing on the front of your feet. This is in contrast to the regular Spiral Dragon standing posture with both feet completely contacting the ground.
Photo by Kaleigh Brown.

Fig. 5.2. Expelling Imbalanced Qi with head and eyes facing left
Photo by Kaleigh Brown.

though they are described individually below. They include movements of hands, feet, head, and eyes.

4. When you feel more comfortable and relaxed, rotate your hands toward the center, palms facing outward with arms at a forty-five-degree angle

Fig. 5.3. Expelling Imbalanced Qi with head and eyes facing right.
Photo by Kaleigh. Brown.

to the ground. Touch your two middle fingers together then move them a few inches apart. This is exactly like the Spiral Dragon Hands exercise described at the beginning of chapter four without pulsing.

5. At the same time that you rotate your palms, raise yourself slightly up on your toes. You only need to elevate your heels an inch or two to raise the ball of your foot from the ground, which is the acupuncture point called *yongquan* or *bubbling spring*, the first point on the Kidney water channel described in chapter three. Balance on your toes so the yongquan point does not touch the ground (Figure 5.1).

6. Also, at the same time rotate your head to the left as far as you can comfortably. Keep your torso facing forward and immoveable. The

movement only involves your neck and head (Figure 5.2). On the next repetition, turn your head to the right (Figure 5.3).

7. While your head is turned as much as you can, rotate your eyes farther to the left. As you become more flexible with practice you may be able to see behind you. When you repeat the exercise with the variation of moving your head right, move your eyes right also. In both left and right versions, you are looking over your shoulders without turning your spine. As you rotate your eyes to their maximum, you will experience a fierceness that expels negative qi. That fierceness is like the gaze of a tiger ready to defend itself.
8. As you combine the motions of rotating your palms toward the center, balancing on your toes, and moving your head then eyes left, hold, then count to seven, fourteen, or twenty-one. In the beginning, counting to seven is sufficient. You need to judge your limits while performing the exercise so you experience feeling better and stronger. You can increase your holding count as you increase number of repetitions.
9. At the end of counting, return to the position of standing on your feet at shoulder's length with palms rotated back outward and then facing the ground. Relax and breathe easily.
10. Repeat all the parts of this exercise together on the left side then followed by the right side. One left and one right repetition together constitute one set. Repeat sets three, seven, fourteen, or twenty-one times. Practice this until you feel better.

This exercise of expelling imbalanced qi is usually more intense than the regular Spiral Dragon sequence. Because of this, take your time to relax between each repetition. If you count to seven while holding the coordinated movements, count at least to fourteen as you relax. The exact number of seconds you rest and relax is not as important as letting go of any tension you experienced during the expelling exercise before you begin the next iteration. If you lose your balance while doing this exercise, don't worry because it is likely. There are five places in the body at which qi moves in and out more rapidly: the back of the skull, the centers of both palms, and the balls of both feet. The expelling exercise simultaneously stimulates these five places, causing negative qi to flow out more forcefully as it is replaced instantly by purified qi. This quick movement of qi through the body may cause imbalance. If you do experience imbalance while raised up on your toes, it is a positive sign that the expelling exercise is working perfectly. Another sign that imbalanced qi has been expelled is that you will notice that your palms, soles of your feet, or back of your neck may become damp with sweat. This sensation also can occur when practicing exercises from the regular sequence of Spiral Dragon. How intensely you experience this sign indicates how quickly and completely you are dispelling dysfunctional qi from your system.

Pointed Focus: Standing or Sitting

The main principle of Spiral Dragon is working with your body, emotions, energy, and awareness exactly as you find them in the present moment. Some days you are bright and active, some days, you may feel duller and more lethargic. The rhythm of living is constant fluctuation. Chapters four and five presented the ideal of stable practice at which you will become skilled, like riding a bicycle. Learning to ride means learning the individual skills of mounting and dismounting, balance, pedaling forward, steering, and braking. Later you learn to execute different tricks and shortcuts that seemed daunting on day one. You shape your riding experiences differently if you are sightseeing, exercising, completing errands, racing, or darting off on a quick departure. As you learn to perform all five exercises and meditation with confidence acquired from a few weeks of steady practice, you are ready to incorporate moment-to-moment awareness of your actual experience.

To elevate your Spiral Dragon practice to the next level, keep your mind focused at the spinal center at your navel chakra during each exercise. This is the same as the instruction for Spiral Dragon Meditation. Apply that meditative focus continuously as you perform each of the five moving exercises whether standing or sitting. This focus will help you connect more completely with the flows of energy throughout your entire body and aura. Like the meditation, whenever you become distracted, simply return your attention to your navel and continue the exercise from where you were. As you practice, whenever you need to scan your body to check your state of relaxation, move your attention to wherever you feel tension or discomfort. After you release any tension you discover, re-center your focus at the navel. You will find that as you become more skilled at maintaining focus while moving, you will discover that it is much, much easier to focus during Spiral Dragon Meditation.

Even though Spiral Dragon is a way to achieve deeper levels of relaxation, ironically, practitioners become tired doing so. Rather than stop altogether, you can shift your practice into energetic pause which is described later below, or you can continue to practice from a sitting posture instead of standing. Especially during the first month of practicing Spiral Dragon, you may find it difficult to stand through all five exercises, so you may sit in the chair you've placed behind you to practice. The sitting practice posture is slightly different from the one described in the previous chapter for meditation.

Exercise

SPIRAL DRAGON SITTING POSTURE

1. Sit at the front of the chair keeping your spine upright.
2. Place your feet on the ground parallel to one another, shoulder-width apart with toes pointing straight ahead (Figure 5.4).
3. Perform any of the five moving exercises from this posture. It will be more restrictive than standing, but it is important for you to compare how sitting versus standing effects the movement of internal energy.
4. When ready, stand up and resume practice from where you left off.

Some days you may decide to alternate sitting and standing during the entire Spiral Dragon practice session.

Fig. 5.4. Performing Spiral Dragon from a chair.
Photo by Kaleigh Brown.

Sudden Depletion

Often during Spiral Dragon practice sessions, Master Quan would ask students what they experienced. His insight broadened our understanding and often gave us ways to attune our practice more precisely. One day a man complained that he felt hollow, empty, tired, and suddenly drained of energy. Instead of feeling more energetic from practicing Spiral Dragon, he experienced the exact opposite. That was the first time I heard of this condition. Here I will combine many commentaries on this subject into a single discussion.

Master Quan first became aware of this condition when teaching in Shanghai in the 1980s. It was a rare occurrence among his students that involved their energy suddenly disappearing. By the time he was teaching in Seattle in the early 1990s, this happened to about a tenth of his students. By the late 1990s when teaching in the San Jose, California, area, Master Quan discovered that the hollowed-out, depleted condition was occurring even more often to students.

The depletion experience had changed over time from occurring mostly during Spiral Dragon practice, to occurring more often in everyday life moments like at a meal or while reading. That's how I became aware of it personally. I didn't experience a feeling of becoming slowly drained, rather it was instantaneous recognition of what already happened. Sometimes I was directly aware of it, but sometimes another person's observation made me indirectly aware. I would find myself without energy, spacey, staring at nothing in particular, and definitely disconnected and drained from what I was doing just moments earlier. Master Quan attributed the phenomenon primarily to a collective structure of karma accumulating around Earth. This energy structure has been aggregating the results of human selfish versus altruistic actions for ages while gathering greater attractive force. Secondarily, the karma structure is influenced by the eleven-year solar sunspot cycle, by the eclipse cycle of a little less than nineteen years, and by the dynamics of planetary alignments. At some future measured in years or decades, the structure will release the energy it has held, saturating Earth in what has become a net negative accumulation. In the meantime, it will continue to deplete the human energetic field increasingly.

The practical question Master Quan investigated was how to counter the effects of sudden depletion whether it occurred during Spiral Dragon or daily life. In a year-long experiment, Master Quan's students were both the subjects and beneficiaries. The solution that worked the best to recover depleted life force is the following simple ritual.

Exercise

ENERGY BODY QI RETRIEVAL EXERCISE

1. Repeat your name three times followed by reciting a short mantra seven times. That makes a round of ten separate recitations. Repeat rounds in sets of three, seven, fourteen, or twenty-one times until you can feel your energy return.
2. The name you choose to recite audibly can be your nickname, a first name, or your entire given name. What is more effective is to recite a spiritual initiation name if you have one. It need not be Buddhist or tantric, but can be from any spiritual tradition with which you identify strongly. If that name is secret, you need to protect its secrecy by thinking or reciting your name inaudibly. Experiment to see which name works better for you.
3. After your name, chant the mantra: **AUM GA JI_U SHU HO!** It should be recited deliberately, sounding each vowel as: **AOUUMM, GA JEE-UUU, SHU HO**. Take your time reciting your name and mantra together. Often, you will be able to feel your energy refresh as you chant.
4. When you prove to yourself that this ritual works, you can help other people recover their lost energy with greater intensity. Join them in their audible chanting using their name and the mantra. This is helpful for aiding children or someone who is ill and has experienced sudden energy depletion.

This practice is a life force retrieval ritual similar in effect to what some traditions teach as soul retrieval. From the Spiral Dragon Dharma perspective, you are not recovering your soul, but rather your energy and its reintegration into your energy body. Over the normal course of your life, your qi may have been lost or fragmented in any number of ways. You may have depleted your qi pursuing work or career. Your qi may have been stolen intentionally by predatory beings, or you may have burnt yourself out fulfilling too many obligations. However your life force may have been dissipated, you are able to recall it immediately. It doesn't matter how long ago it was lost or taken; since it belongs to you, your energy will return when you call it home with this ritual. This mantra provides an easy method to reignite, reenergize, and refresh yourself quickly, and can be practiced easily outside Spiral Dragon sessions.

Energetic Pause

In the middle of practicing Spiral Dragon, you might notice that you are more tired than you initially thought. Rather than interrupting your practice to rest, you can rest within the practice. This amounts to shifting yourself into a neutral state so you can continue to relax easily for as many minutes as it takes you to become ready to return to practice. You can do this from a standing or sitting posture as described above. By using this pause, you do not need to start all over again, but rather continue to retain the momentum your earlier practice created.

Exercise

PERFORMING ENERGETIC PAUSE TO CONSERVE YOUR ENERGY

1. Put your right hand over your left by specifically circling your right thumb and index finger around your left wrist. This also aligns the centers of both palms, right above left.
2. Then, put both hands on your navel as shown in Figure 5.5.
3. Make sure you hold your arms a few inches away from your torso so that energy can continue to freely circulate.
4. Place your attention at your navel until you are ready to resume Spiral Dragon.

Restoring Your Health and Energy ∽ 73

Fig. 5.5. Alternate hand mudra for conserving
energy, resting, or meditation.
Photo by Kaleigh Brown.

There are two other applications for the above mudra hand position, one in meditation and one in daily life. As you meditate, some days you may recognize that your thoughts or emotions bounce more wildly about, not slowing or settling down. In place of the hand mudra usually used for Spiral Dragon Meditation, you can join both hands at the navel as just described. This later mudra makes a stronger energetic connection so you can focus attention at your navel more palpably and easily. When you notice that your thoughts and emotions have subsided enough, you can change your hand posture back to the main meditation mudra. The second application is useful whenever you find yourself in a hostile place or in company with unsettling people. It is especially useful for anyone who is very sensitive or subject to strong anxieties. Whether sitting or standing, put your hands over your navel as shown above. It is a posture that won't draw undue notice. It has the benefit of protecting you as you conserve your energy safely within. It's an especially useful posture to maintain until you can excuse yourself from any negativity you may sense, and then move away comfortably.

Practicing in Health Extremes

There are extremes of health when you need to lie in bed on your back or your side because any other posture is painful. Sometimes you may barely have the strength to sit up in a chair or in bed. Even in those circumstances you can perform parts of Spiral Dragon from a posture laying on your back. In daily life, we don't do spiritual practice laying down because it's too easy to doze off to sleep. When you're very ill, that's not a problem. You can always do the very first Relax exercise described in chapter three from any posture. In fact, if you have a lot of bodily pain, discomfort, or tension, directing your awareness to the place of pain can bring release and relief. You have to be willing to face your condition and allow yourself to explore the condition as you find it without judging. That determination alone requires a certain amount of courage, but also contains the necessary means to release pain and restore health. Determination, patience and the skill of using your awareness with the sound of the **HA** syllable is the essence of powerful healing at the center of the Spiral Dragon system.

Restoring Health and Energy Is Restoring Enlightenment

Body, energy, and mind interdepend upon each another. In doing any spiritual practice, sometimes it is easier to release obstacles to enlightenment from your body, sometimes from your energy field, and sometimes from your awareness. When you release obscuring obstacles, you realize the primordial condition of enlightenment which is and has always been present. Playing and practicing with Spiral Dragon reveals where it is both easiest and most effective to release obstacles including pain, afflictive emotions, or obsessive thinking. The more you place yourself at ease in the dynamic and spontaneous awareness of Spiral Dragon, the easier it is to recognize and allow all the knots in your body, energy flows, and mind to untangle by themselves.

> *The Tao is so empty*
> *those who use it*
> *never become full again*
> *and so deep*
> *as if it were the ancestor of us all*
> *dulling our edges*
> *untying our tangles*
> *softening our light*
> *merging our dust*
> *and so clear*
> *as if it were present*
> *I wonder whose child it is*
> *It seems it was here before Ti**
>
> TAOTECHING, 4TH VERSE,
> RED PINE TRANSLATION.[1]

---

*Ti is the supreme creator god of Chinese philosophy. Ti is also referred to as Shang⁴ di⁴ (上帝) or Huang² tian¹ Shang⁴ di⁴ (皇天上帝).

6

Creative Play and Progress
Rhythms of Spiral Dragon

In the last three chapters, we have considered how to engage in the practice of Spiral Dragon exercise by exercise. We have examined in detail pieces of the practice. In this chapter, we look more generally at Spiral Dragon play in the course of a single session and consider integrating it over time into your regular life routine. As mentioned in the introduction, you may consider this chapter to be more about launching the trajectory of your Spiral Dragon experience. I have grouped common questions and concerns students have voiced over the last thirty-plus years into themes.

Recommended Practice Length for Sessions

How long should you practice Spiral Dragon in a session? The fast response is to practice in one continuous session on average from fifty to sixty-five minutes starting at the Relax exercise and ending when meditation is over. That is an average that doesn't really address what Spiral Dragon is all about, which is transforming and integrating your body, energy, and awareness. Your actual experience is the real measure of how long you personally should practice, and that length of time may vary some from day to day. It may be more or less than an hour. After a week of playing with Spiral Dragon you will have some experiences of how you feel. What you want to recognize is the moment your energy seems to shift up a level. Although it is not as dramatic nor disorienting as receiving a slight electric shock, you will easily be able to recognize it. From that up-shift moment, you should practice another five or ten minutes. Total practice time includes meditation, but it is better to meditate after you have experienced the up-shift to the Spiral Dragon dynamic.

Master Quan made the analogy between Spiral Dragon practice and cooking rice. When cooking rice, it is necessary to raise the water temperature to boiling so raw rice will begin to transform into an edible and tasty meal. If the water never boils, or if the raw rice grains do not cook long enough, you will have made a milky slush and not a nutritious meal. Your cooking effort will have been wasted. We each are like raw rice grains. When we fail to increase our inner fire sufficiently or for long enough, we will not achieve a useful result. The moral is to be patient enough in practice to realize fully the benefits for all your precious effort. Ultimately, you are the only one who can experience whether or not your energy level rises to the transition state in which you spontaneously transform on any given day.

Timeframes for Differing Stages of Accomplishment

At each stage of Spiral Dragon practice, there are signs of accomplishment. A majority of people who initially learn Spiral Dragon over the course of two to six hours of training have profound experiences. One example is I taught a day-long course in feng shui to interior designers, which included an hour of Spiral Dragon practice. The goal was for the attendees to learn to feel the qi of place as a way to work with household spaces. At the break, an older interior designer said she had come to learn about feng shui, but the unexpected and best benefit of the day was that she was free of her arthritic pain for the first time in eight years. I advised her to practice the Spiral Dragon we learned that day to keep her arthritis at bay. Many people experience profound insights at the beginning. Furthermore, within the first three days of Spiral Dragon, most students usually have clear and vivid dreams. If you do, record them in a journal for later review. The main and necessary sign as discussed in chapter three is that after doing Relax and Sky Dragon exercises, you experience spontaneous swaying of your body. Another way of describing this phenomenon is that you feel successive waves moving through your physical body, energy body, and mind. This means that you have connected with a realm of energy beyond local space and time, and that will accelerate all your subsequent practice. It will accelerate your life's mission. It will accelerate your enlightenment.

Depending on how consistently you practice, within two weeks to one month you will have learned most of the mechanics, procedures, and variations of Spiral Dragon so that it ceases being a deliberate effort and becomes more familiar play. You will also have experienced the arising of spontaneous body movements that can seem like anything from a blend of several Spiral Dragon postures, dance, taiji, sport moves, or completely new movements for you. The way to work with these movements is to let them arise, but when they've played themselves out, return to what you were practicing before the spontaneity occurred. This is also the period when you try more involved Spiral Dragon experiments. For example, your lower back may ache, so you determine to test Spiral Dragon Palms systematically. How much will it really lessen your lower back pain and improve your overall health? This Spiral Dragon phase launches a more extensive exploration of the universe of your own experience led by your own inquisitiveness and persistence.

As you play with Spiral Dragon over several months, more and more you recognize the interplay of a guiding intelligence. Without thinking or asking, you are prompted with insight. It leads you to connect a few threads that might include something you learned at age eleven with an interesting conversation you may have had yesterday with a food you should eat to improve your health. This is the intelligence of infinite interconnection at play. The more you immerse yourself in Spiral Dragon, the deeper and more frequent you have ah-ha moments, both practical and galactic. As moments of astonishing insight arise increasingly during your waking and dreaming hours, it is a very reliable sign that you are practicing Spiral Dragon well. Once you have confidence from reflecting on the signs and positive transformation you have experienced since learning and regularly engaging in Spiral Dragon, you are ready to commit to the next phase.

Ninety Days of Spiral Dragon

In the example of cooking rice, it is all about activating a high enough temperature for long enough to create a nourishing meal on that one day. Our human energy system when heated continuously over longer periods of time precipitates quantum level changes in our body-energy-mind complexes which shift potential skills into active skills. These shifts also lead to sudden and spontaneous increases in awareness, intelligence, and realization of enlightenment. The next phase change occurs as a result of practicing Spiral Dragon every day without a break for ninety days, the length of one season. This creates an increasing skill base with which you become more familiar, facile, and competent while establishing your energy field in a more even, harmonious dynamic. On a practical level, you will be more readily able to pick up exactly where you stopped exploring yesterday.

Ninety days of continuous Spiral Dragon allows you more easily and frequently to connect and maintain the frequency of the spiral dynamic. This both conserves and increases the momentum of personal transformation that you are generating through Spiral Dragon. It doesn't matter if your goal is to accelerate your life purpose and mission, to achieve enlightenment, or both. This is an essential activation step. It was so important that Master Quan considered ninety practice days as a minimum for a student or disciple to become sufficiently experienced to teach Spiral Dragon to others.

Individual Differences in Signs and Experiences

At the beginning of chapter one, we discussed how each person has individual karmas that color their path to reawakening in enlightenment. The Buddha discussed 84,000 different pathways to enlightenment. Within these 84,000 paths, there are many important individual differences even when someone resonates very highly with a particular path. This is evident in a group of people who all learn Spiral Dragon together for the first time and continue practice regularly after that. When asked about their significant experiences from a particular day, or personal insights recurring over months, they each report a different set and sequence of important moments for them. This means that you should not compare your practice too closely with others. Signs of connection and accomplishment will arise according to the unique karmic way your body, energy, and mind came together, and how you are managing your life. The path back to both happiness and enlightenment is not by adding what we think we lack. Rather, the return path is by releasing whatever most distresses us and is ready for release first. It may be physical, emotional, energetic, or mental. Release happens naturally and by itself whenever we place our relaxed awareness unwaveringly on any knot of tension which we find present. Ultimately, our distresses have scattered and fragmented us causing fundamental unhappiness. However, each time we release some difficulty we reintegrate and return to our inherent sense of wholeness. This liberating process happens over and over as we recover our life purpose and mind of enlightenment in stable realization. Spiral Dragon accelerates this natural process uniquely for each of us.

One day during group practice, a student asked Master Quan about long term Spiral Dragon progress. He laughed and replied that it is as if most of us were just practicing in the front yard of a great three-story house. We hadn't yet gotten through the front door of the house, nor even noticed the three floors of the house in front us representing possible levels of unexplored experience.

Conditions for Unconditioned Spiral Dragon

Many of Master Quan's students had seriously practiced taiji, one or more forms of qi gong, and/or other yogic, Daoist, Confucian, or Buddhist disciplines. Some of these practices come with very specific sets of directions about how to maximize practice depending on personal circumstances. This section is more for readers who have similar concerns. As you consider the comparisons, it will highlight the uniqueness of Spiral Dragon. Echoing explanations from earlier chapters, Spiral Dragon opens the gate of dynamic connection with the universe that lies beyond the time/space coordinates in which we practice. Once you make and maintain that connection, everything else arises naturally and does not benefit from extra ritual. To practice Spiral Dragon is to step into the infinite. Nonetheless, I will pass on the answers Master Quan gave about favorable practice conditions.

A common concern is whether men and women have different practice instructions. Though this is the case in some qi gong practices, it is not necessary for Spiral Dragon. Energy flows do usually circulate in opposite directions for men and women in right or left spins. During Spiral Dragon practice, the energies spontaneously can and do move in both directions for men and women. More importantly, energies become more serene and flows become more continuously steady within the plane of the physical body for all practitioners. The energy flows also begin to activate more of the meridians surrounding the body. Only twelve or fewer of the potential 108,000 extra corporeal meridians are activated in the average adult human, or just one ten-thousandth of one percent. When even one-ninth, or about twelve thousand outer meridians, are charged and begin to flow after sitting dormant since birth, that qi circulation produces dramatic change. This major shift creates a new and substantial integration of outer, inner, and central meridian network flows. Allowing Spiral Dragon to adjust the energy flowing at the moment is necessary for both women and men.

Place and Time of Day

Because Spiral Dragon does open connections to other time/space coordinates, the particulars of when and where you practice have the most effect when you begin Spiral Dragon. After that they diminish as a concern. At the start, being in a nourishing environment is very helpful. If inside, lighting a candle and offering incense at your personal altar or usual spiritual practice place clears and purifies your practice space making it more harmonious as a support. Then connect mentally with Senton Dorje and Master Quan by offering a prayer or intention. You can use the ritual of placing your left palm facing outward at the heart level and right palm facing upward directly below your navel. The right palm generates protection while the left receives active blessings (Figure 6.1). You can intensify this by mirroring your

Fig. 6.1. Both hands mudra of receiving blessings.
Photo by Kaleigh Brown.

Fig. 6.2. Master Quan's Life Torch Bodhi Temple.

hand while viewing the image of Master Quan's transmitting hand in Figure 3.1 (page 34). As you look at the image of Master Quan's Life Torch Bodhi Temple (Figure 6.2 above), you can also visualize yourself in the palpable presence of the lineage source of Spiral Dragon dharma.

You may feel more comfortable practicing outdoors and may find that you can connect more easily with the vast sky you see and feel. You ought to avoid practicing in places that are physically toxic or polluted. This includes avoiding practice near places where you can sense strong negative emotions. As you become more skilled at Spiral Dragon, you will be able to connect to other positive time/space energies and draw them into circulation wherever you are.

The time of day you practice is not as important as that you do practice every day. We each have particular circadian rhythms, times in the daily cycle when we are duller or sharper. When learning Spiral

Dragon, it may be better to practice during one of your natural daily up-cycles. If you can't practice at that time due to your schedule, practicing Spiral Dragon even at your lower ebb moments will still replenish your energy. A twenty-four-hour day has twelve two-hour cycles each favoring a ruling element and activating an organ system, but it is not necessary to choose one consciously for practice. More broadly there are the two halves of a day, light and dark. Follow your intuition in picking either daylight or night, but eventually experiment with both for practice. The other half-day division you may find more useful. In the twelve hours from six a.m. to six p.m., energies saturate your physical body more making it ideal for physical exercise, training, and work. In the opposite period, from six p.m. to six a.m., energies saturate your energy body more making it ideal for inspiration, quiet study, and creative projects. Depending on your goal, choose moments in the half day to play with Spiral Dragon energies. A flaw of modern life is that there are so many artificial rhythms constraining our free choice actions. Be practical to use and explore the best time you have available.

Cardinal Directions

Facing a particular direction is often paired with time-of-day injunctions for a wide variety of inner cultivation practices. East at dawn, south at noon, west at sunset, or north at midnight are common schemes. With Spiral Dragon, none of these prescriptions are necessary, but over time you may want to experiment with each of them to verify what you may find. An interesting experiment is to practice with your eyes closed so that you do not visually anchor yourself to a direction or to a major feature in the surrounding landscape like a snow-capped mountain. When you finally do open your eyes, you can see if or where you have rotated. Is there some magnetic quality in your local environment, literally or figuratively, that you are engaging or that is calibrating you?

Facing north is a common and important orientation in many

rituals and inner alchemy practices. This is because magnetic north is the directional attractor for all life kingdoms. The north view of the pole star at night reveals the stable center of Earth's rotation. The axis of rotation has been compared to the central world tree or world mountain in myth and ancient teachings. That makes it the recognized center for all of us. Approaching the center, however we accomplish that by ritual or visualization, is the act of harmonizing with every part of the cosmos. I can add here that doing the Relax and Sky Dragon exercises encompasses the equivalent essence of this ritual no matter which direction you face in the local environment.

We also can explore our connection with planetary and galactic magnetism through Spiral Dragon, paying attention to internal and external conditions. Usually a stable feature, Earth's magnetic forces have become more erratic since 1859.[1] The Earth's magnetic field is now weakening at an accelerating rate. Independent of, but exacerbating Earth's magnetic stability, is the eleven-year sunspot cycle. As Master Quan taught Spiral Dragon in the late 1990's, Solar Cycle 23 increased in activity producing larger Coronal Mass Ejections (CMEs), geomagnetic storms, and X-ray flares. These sun-Earth electromagnetic and atmospheric changes were felt by the Spiral Dragon students who reacted to these phenomena. The only consistent pattern was that sudden depletion became prevalent for more students. Master Quan encouraged each of us to experiment to determine which phenomena most affected us and how. He wanted us to pay attention through the lens of our experiences as opposed to checking in first with NOAA* for the latest space weather statistics. He also wanted us to test what we could do to create inner balance or outer balance after observing what these solar phenomena actually produced in our bodies, emotions, and mind streams.

---

*National Oceanic and Atmospheric Administration.

Engaging Spiral Dragon Insight

During the course of your practice, you will become aware of actionable intelligence, some with immediate application to your life. You will be inspired to take direct action for yourself or others. For instance, you might become aware that you need to discover how well your body is actually assimilating calcium as this may be an important health issue for you. Once that awareness arises at different moments and in different contexts, you need to act on this deep intuition. Of course, in the beginning, you must test to see if your Spiral Dragon insights prove to provide valid information. Once you begin to see that your actionable awareness is true, you can begin to rely more on the inner intelligence surfacing to guide you. This is an important sign as you begin to meet, test, and rely on your inner guru, the source of profound and true direction.

Next, more complicated intelligence arises at the overlapping boundaries of your inner and outer worlds. You may encounter the solar and terrestrial magnetic cycles we discussed above, as ideas, as visceral experience, and as Spiral Dragon play. Do you need to engage that awareness usefully? In discussing Solar Cycle 23, Master Quan saw intensification of the sunspot cycle as the critical period in which collective humanity would precipitously rise or fall. As an example of the increased outer intensity of Solar Cycle 23, forty of the fifty greatest solar flares erupted then.[2] As a response to strengthen the field of compassionate action, we collectively practiced specific mantras together. Some students perceived that their longer-term actionable intelligence was to improve their skills at healing while others wanted to investigate what sunspot Solar Cycle 23 was actually creating. Later, each would investigate what learning and skills they could develop to engage in more effective positive action.

The most profound intuitions that arise have to do with guiding your life purpose and how you can manifest that as your main life mission. When this level of inner guiding intelligence arises, it leads you to express your life path as your central priority. This creates inner and outer synergy releasing lifelong tension that has accumulated from resisting or being unable to fulfill your life's purpose. You may or may not have needed Spiral Dragon to get to this point in your life. In the next chapter, we will explore how you can apply Spiral Dragon exercises to develop skills that express your enthusiastic interests. We will also consider how you can play with Spiral Dragon to manifest your life purpose as your dharma path.

7

Refining Your Destiny
Signs in the Hands

One day, Master Quan was teaching Spiral Dragon to a group of students. The conversation had turned to a discussion of places Master Quan had lived after moving to the United States: Seattle, metropolitan Los Angeles, and the Bay Area of Northern California. Someone asked him the question of why he decided to stay in the Bay Area. He replied that it was the difference in geography, specifically the tectonic substrate of both California areas. This was the reason he chose to live in Northern California. When he stayed at Hsi Lai Temple in Hacienda Heights in the greater Los Angeles area, he experimented with the nearby San Andreas and lesser geologic faults of Southern California. He was working on a way to release the buildup of geologic stress so that when an earthquake occurred, its Richter scale intensity would be less than if it released energy as a naturally occurring earthquake. When living south of San Francisco, he also experimented with the dynamics of earthquakes. He determined that the underlying fault structure of the Bay Area made it less vulnerable to experiencing an extremely devastating earthquake. The reason he moved north simply was because he could lessen the earthquake danger in Northern California, but not as much in Southern California.

Master Quan did not use any equipment, neither mechanical nor electromagnetic, to release vast amounts of Earth qi. This was an ability he developed over the years as a result of his mastery of Spiral Dragon. When describing the role of Spiral Dragon, he described it as an engine that drives other higher-level practices. It is easy for me to attest to his ability because there was a stream of earthquakes that occurred in the Bay Area that I experienced. Later I learned through discussions with Master Quan he had sensed them beforehand and pointed out to me the conditions before the quake and the resulting registered magnitude. He described the fault system from Silicon Valley branching in both directions around the bay. Master Quan did consult maps, but he relied on his own primary investigation of the substrate. He even discovered extra fault lines that weren't published until later. He further described that the build-up of tectonic stress before an earthquake could not be released until the earthquake began to activate. For that he had to know what was about to happen and then divert the major portion of the energy harmlessly into the atmosphere as the earthquake began.

When teaching Spiral Dragon, Master Quan did address the topic of great earthquakes regularly because in his view, this would become an increasingly dangerous threat. He openly stated he wanted some of his students to develop this same ability through Spiral Dragon, thus serving as Earth protectors. Some students thought he was exaggerating, but I found him to be very serious and matter of fact about this. I remembering him discussing great earthquakes to come that would register 9.0 and above on the Richter scale. He pointed out how we do have the ability to reduce the effects of a 9.5 to a 5.5 scale quake. I remarked: "We can live with that!" He replied nodding: "We can live with that."

Master Quan had also developed healing abilities to an extraordinary level. His view was that you cannot be a dharma teacher without being able to heal others. His father was a qi gong master, acupuncturist, and herbalist who trained him thoroughly from a young age, so Master Quan had a natural and learned affinity to the healing arts. People sought Master Quan's healing especially when other conventional medicines, including Western allopathic medicine and TCM, had not generated a cure. When people came to him for healing, he would scan them, then draw a picture of the area of their body that was diseased. If they had medical imaging, he asked to see it after he imaged their condition himself. The two versions often confirmed one another. If his students were present at a healing session, he would ask them what they had sensed during the healing, but only after the patient had responded. He would include some of that insight to explain the patient's health issue and what the patient could do for continued healing. If pertinent, Master Quan would describe how the health situation developed from one of their past lifetimes and prescribe a mantra for them to chant.

One day a Chinese man asked for a healing. He was experiencing excruciating pain at the spine behind his heart, a very sharp pain that came and went. Master Quan directed the man to lie face down on the floor. Usually, Master Quan had the patient sit in a chair while he sat in a nearby chair. Someone walking into a healing session would observe Master Quan sitting quietly, sometimes in motionless meditation, sometimes moving his hands through a series of mudras conducting energy. On this occasion, Master Quan stood over the man, moving his hands in mudras, and occasionally questioning him. At the conclusion of a long session, he asked the man what percent improvement he was feeling. The answer was only thirty percent better, so Master Quan gave him some advice on what he could do to continue healing. After the man left, Master Quan explained to me what happened as the discussion had been in Mandarin. He also provided more esoteric background.

In a past life, the patient had stabbed another man in the back. The place where the patient experienced his excruciating pain was exactly the same place the patient had thrust a deadly spearpoint to kill another in that former life. Master Quan said the reason he could not bring about a more thorough cure at that moment was that the patient still had afflictive hate in his heart for his former victim. In order to heal, the patient would need to release that emotion completely and regret his negative act. Master Quan added that when he healed people earlier in his career, he had tried to dissolve the karmic causes that his patients had generated that were ultimately responsible for their diseases in this life. As he had never become completely successful at this, he realized that for healing to happen, patients needed a change of heart to release their sufferings. What Master Quan could do for patients who resisted the change of heart during a healing session with him was to embed a packet of energy and information in their energy stream that would open to help them when they regretted and released negative past life causes. This is exactly the strategy he used with the man in excruciating back pain. At some moment in this or a future life, if the patient replaced negativity with compassion, he would then and there become aware of how to affect his own healing completely. Master Quan's healing dynamic would continue through time and space following this patient through incarnation after incarnation until this healing became a future cure.

On another occasion, Master Quan described to me the highest form of healing as a thought experiment. He said that suppose a seventy-year-old man came to him to help heal a painful stomach condition. He might scan the patient's condition and determine that within a few years he would die from this malady because his stomach disease was beyond curability. Instead of trying merely to bring this gentleman relief in the present, Master Quan might use a different method. He could regress the patient's stomach complex backward through time to when he was only nineteen, a time just before his stomach had become diseased. Then Master Quan could progress his healthy stomach-state through time to his present age and replace the diseased stomach. The patient now would be well with an aged but healthy stomach. I was stunned not because of the thought experiment, but because I knew Master Quan was using this healing method when he could. I blurted out: "The disease never happened!" He looked at me incisively and said: "It never happened." He added this level of healing is possible for anyone to achieve, and that the sure path to it is through Spiral Dragon.

Spiral Power Moving Through Your Spine and Hands

We are limited by our perceptions and beliefs. When you play with Spiral Dragon, you immerse yourself in a continuous state of primordial

Figs. 7.1–7.5. Spiral Dragon hands series.
Photos by Kaleigh Brown.

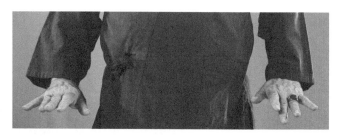

Earth palms mudra.

Rotated palms mudra.

Closed fingers mudra.

Palms facing mudra.

Meditation mudra.

energy and awareness. In this state phenomenal abilities arise, partly of themselves, partly because the world needs them from you, and partly from your dedicated investigation and practice. The root of access is the very first two exercises of Relax and Sky Dragon which many people powerfully experience in their very first Spiral Dragon session. As you open your spine, you connect to the infinite flow of spiral energies throughout the cosmos. Your natural awareness will open the realm of your potential abilities. How you shape your latent abilities from then on has to do with your hands and mind.

The body has many microsystems such as the ear, tongue, hand, and foot each of which is a map of the whole body. They each holistically contain access to all the corresponding parts of the body. These microsystems are useful especially when an area or acupuncture point is too painful to touch directly. Instead, you simply activate healing through the microsystem correspondences. All the microsystems have the capacity to restore your body to the highest health fitness you ever have experienced in this lifetime. The Korean Koryo microsystem of the hands, however, is different in that activating healing through your hands can elevate you above your highest health fitness. We have discussed this but it is essential to remember and consciously engage. Spiral Dragon emphasizes the catalyzing flow of energy through a series of various hand postures. When you consider the whole flow of images above of Spiral Dragon hand mudras (Figures 7.1 through 7.5), you will see a hand ballet in the series of five natural, very compact movements.

Signs in the Hands

Over the course of months of Spiral Dragon play, your hands will register short and long-term changes most noticeably. In the short term, your hands will temporarily turn a redder hue than normal for you. A second, short-term sign is that your palms will show temporary lighter blotches visually, usually accompanied by feeling heat and tingling in your hands. See Figure 7.6 on page 94. Master Quan taught that each temporary blotch appearing on your palm indicates that you have connected with a particular star's

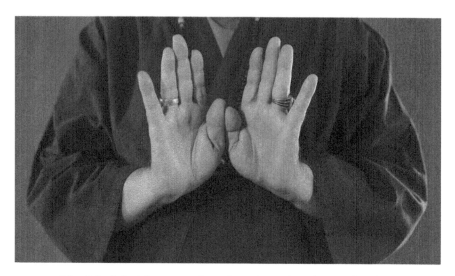

Fig. 7.6. Spiral Dragon, signs in palms showing activation.
Photo by Kaleigh Brown.

energy. More blotches indicate more connected stars! Longer-term changes happen as the lines in your palms shift and change, which means that your karma is altering. At the beginning of Spiral Dragon, take photos of your palms to compare with the actual state of your palms at three-month intervals. Often, I would walk into a room and find Master Quan examining the state of his palms in rapt detail. He told me that was one way he monitored changes in his karma and the karma of his students.

As you play with Spiral Dragon, you will be able to recognize when you are experiencing the open system of primordial energy whether you are practicing formally or not. The signs are many, but principally, your spine seems energized, your mind is making rapid connections you didn't see before, and your hands are glowing. One of the stronger instances of this for me occurred when I was preoccupied examining diamonds and rubies in the presence of tens of thousands of other precious gems at the Tucson Gem and Mineral Show. I thanked a vendor, and as I went to shake his hand, my hands were fiery red. They had never been that color before, and pulsed with intense energy. The vendor joked that I should buy his entire stock because of my visible change. In those moments, you can question and experiment with any aspects of life and it will lead to brilliant insights. This is when you apply Spiral Dragon to ignite your potentials and skills.

Exercises to Apply Spiral Dragon to Manifest Your Life Interests

Whether you are actively or passively practicing Spiral Dragon, you can gather information through the motion of your hands. You can send and receive information through your palms, but the response may arise through any of the five senses or the mind. Next are two exercises you can do to increase your ability to connect with and learn from objects and phenomena near and far.

Exercise

PULSING YOUR PALMS TO EARTH

1. Stand as in the very first Relax exercise with your feet pointing forward and shoulder-length apart. Place your arms at your sides with palms facing Earth. This is the first position, and it is powerful in itself. The irony is that it is so common that you will have stood automatically in this posture many times naturally throughout your whole life.
2. In all the hand exercises discussed in chapter four, you felt then pulsed magnetism through your palms, fingers, and ultimately your whole body/aura complex. Push your palms downward a few inches feeling the slight magnetic resistance generated by the Earth. Release, then pull upward a few inches still feeling that magnetism.
3. As you push and pull feeling magnetic flow, you will begin to relax more deeply. This same motion also grounds you so it is easier to let go of pestering aches, emotions, and thoughts. This is pulsing without inquiry. See Figures 7.7 and 7.8 on the following page.

4. To make an inquiry all you do is formulate it in your mind, and pulse your palms pushing and pulling energy. As before it is best done in three, seven, or fourteen sets of twenty-one push-pull repetitions.
5. In the beginning of making inquiries, you will have increased success if you ask questions relating to the immediate environment, such as what you need to do to help the nearby crepe myrtle flourish. If you are at an historical spot, you can ask for more information of what happened there. You will probably get information or insights not in the public historical narrative. You may get details verified by the historical written or oral record, something contradictory or something tangential. What information you do receive is nonetheless important for you.

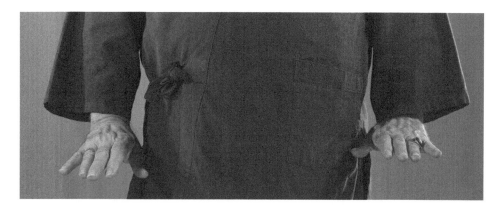

Fig. 7.7. Posture one pulsing energy from the palms to Earth.
Photo by Kaleigh Brown.

Fig. 7.8. Posture two, pulsing energy from the palms to Earth.
Photo by Kaleigh Brown.

I have used the palm pulsing Earth technique to investigate many feng shui details of my home and the homes and properties of clients. An example is a feng shui consultation I did for a couple with several children in a newer home in Arizona. Within the last six months, the wife had asked her mother to move in with the family so she could care for her. The mother, a nurse, had contracted a fatal cancer and was expected to live six months. Her convalescent room was originally designed as a study just off the living room. Unexpectedly, the mother's health deteriorated very rapidly and she died two months after moving in. Among the many questions, most prominent was: What happened? As I checked the energy field of the room, I found it had severely sinking energy which I had only come across once before in a home. The mother's bed was exactly over the middle of this sinking energy field which did not extend outside her room. In this case, it continually drained the qi of the mother whose life force was already at low ebb. Because this was such a unique result, I rechecked several times before reaching certainty. The sinking qi field, though very unusual, was yet a natural anomaly and was present and active as an older Earth energy layer beneath the house.

Exercise

PULSING YOUR PALMS TO A DISTANT OBJECT

1. Once again, stand with your legs apart at shoulder's length and begin with arms at your sides, palms facing Earth.
2. Begin pulsing the magnetic field of the Earth, up and down, for a few minutes, both to relax and to attune your ability to feel magnetism through your palms. It is a brief exercise to calibrate your awareness of the magnetic flow of qi.
3. For this next part, you need to have an object to investigate, whether it is something on a table in front of you or a site farther away in the landscape. There are two parts that follow: connecting, then receiving information.

4. Your palms both pulse and receive energy and information. If you are investigating a small object, use one palm to pulse toward it to connect. Place the other palm at your navel facing up, just like in the meditation hand mudra. See Figure 6.1 in the previous chapter. If you are connecting with a distant object like a tree or the top of a hill, use both palms. If the object is at a distance, raise your arms to your chest level, then extend your arms forward. See Figures 7.9 and 7.10 below. Pulse your palms toward the

Fig. 7.9. Posture one, pulsing energy between the palms and a distant object.
Photo by Kaleigh Brown.

Fig. 7.10. Posture two, pulsing energy between the palms and a distant object.
Photo by Kaleigh Brown.

distant object. Feel the magnetic energy as you push and pull energy. You only need to pulse your palms just a few inches toward the object, then pull back a few inches. If you are connected, just like the Dragon Palms exercise, you will feel both resistance and recoil. Pulse slowly. If you can't feel much, then relax and pulse at a slower pace.

5. At some point you will begin to receive impressions and intuitions. You may also receive information that you can check later, an example being whether a distant house is occupied or vacant. In the beginning, you should allow impressions to freely arise with your mind and body in a relaxed and focused state.

6. Once you become successful at maintaining connection while receiving intuitions, you can direct your information gathering more specifically. You can hold a question lightly in your mind for a few moments, then let go of the question. As you pulse energy, you will get a response, but like having a conversation, you may not find out exactly what you want to know. Also like a conversation with a person, you can follow up with another question, but need to be present and receptive for the response.

Pulsing and Healing

A practical and compassionate use of this pulsing technique is to investigate a variety of health conditions for your immediate circle of family and friends. If a person who is suffering can identify a specific area that is painful, like a sprained ankle, you can pulse energy exactly at that spot. Once you connect and feel the magnetic pulsing, which the patient also often does feel, you will activate an information stream riding upon an energy stream. The information stream may carry insights into how you might pulse more effectively or perhaps provide insight into the underlying condition of the problem, or as in the example, the type of sprain to the ankle. The more thorough your theoretical and practical knowledge is about anatomy and physiology, the more specific will be the types of information you receive and will be able to integrate. Independent of the information stream, the energy connection will automatically begin to activate a healing response in the patient with or without your specific intention or your intellectual understanding of the ailment. The healing side of the energy exchange is spontaneous and dynamically adaptive because it is powered by the spiral universe's expression of natural great perfection.

Another application of pulsing healing is to use it to identify what is disharmonious in any of the human fields of body, emotion, energy, and awareness. In this case, begin pulsing anywhere over or around the patient's body. Allow your hand to slowly move and scan the body. At some places, energy will be stuck, which gives you a chance to explore that area. When unstuck, allow your hand to float along spontaneously on the magnetic field of the patient's aura. See Figure 7.11 below. You will intuit some information and/or you may get the insight to pulse energy at or around a particular area. This description is little more than an invitation to experiment with healing others and see what

Fig. 7.11. Posture for pulsing energy for healing.
Photo by Kaleigh Brown.

happens. There are an indefinite set of healing possibilities which will be meaningful as you allow your energy to engage with the universe as you keep your awareness relaxed, receptive, and focused. As you experiment, you will learn practical skills as well as advance on the path of engaged enlightenment.

By way of disclosure, there is another set of parallel Spiral Dragon exercises that develop specific skills more deeply. To keep this book inspirational, focused, and practical, I am not including a description or instruction of those variations of Spiral Dragon here. They can follow after gaining skill, ease, and confidence in the Spiral Dragon exercises outlined so far. I will, however, conclude with a comment Master Quan made often when teaching and exploring these skill-building variations in this chapter. He would raise the index finger of his right hand and say: "Very useful. Very, very useful!"

8

Mudra, Mantra, and Inner Transformation

Interconnections of Body, Breath, and Mind

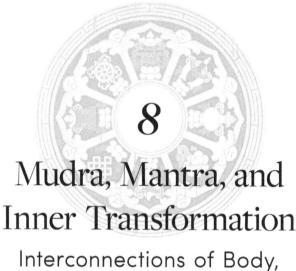

As mentioned earlier, I met Master Quan in Seattle near the end of summer in 1989, and that fall I began to drive him to the Northwest Institute of Acupuncture and Oriental Medicine so he could teach his first course in Spiral Dragon in the United States, which the college loosely advertised as a practice for healers. I was driving a 1968 Volkswagen beetle that was a Frankenstein of mismatched parts. Even the original shift handle had been replaced by a golf ball. As I chauffeured Master Quan about, I was sorry he had to ride about in such a humble-mobile. The other really acute awareness I had was that my right hand on the shift handle spontaneously formed a mudra. It happened every time I drove him. Each time I shifted gears during each trip, my hand would take on the same mudra, one that I hadn't practiced before. Eventually, I would notice my right hand forming this same mudra when I conversed with Master Quan. The important point here is that the new mudra first arose spontaneously before I learned any Spiral Dragon.

The mudra I experienced consists of touching the tips of the thumb and ring fingers together. In Indian yoga, this is referred to as the Prithvi mudra that joins the fire and earth element fingers in a circuit. I've also learned since that different spiritual traditions name this mudra differently with each ascribing a particular set of benefits or outcomes to this practice. With your current familiarity with Spiral Dragon, you can appreciate the importance of hands for connecting and moving the flow of energy through your body or through the environment. Although Master Quan did not explain the science and use of mudras as part of Spiral Dragon, he did teach it in parallel and by demonstration. He favored giving enough information for students to explore Spiral Dragon through their own direct investigation. Any background of theory emerged through his answers to heartfelt questions arising from firsthand experiences. Knowing and using mudras as an extension of Spiral Dragon will arise as you spontaneously engage and conduct qi flow through the circuitry of your own energy meridians.

Mudras

Moving Qi, Light, and Information

Whereas mantras circulate and synchronize geometries of sound, mudras circulate and synchronize geometries of qi, light, and information. Mudra can be defined as *gesture* especially when it refers to hands, but it can be extended to include all body postures including the asanas of Daoist and Hatha Yogas. It is logical that changing the circuitry of posture will influence the circulation of all types of energy through the body and aura. Hand gestures are particularly potent in Spiral Dragon for receiving and transmitting energy because of the preeminence of the hand microsystem in inner transformation and healing. There are two types of mudras you will encounter. The first group arises spontaneously from practice, whereas the second type is from traditionally practiced mudras. Though both types create energetic synergies, spontaneous mudras have the advantage of arising as personal tools to purify challenging karma and accelerate accomplishment of your potential destiny.

The root mudra is the Spiral Dragon Meditation mudra of joined hands described in chapter four, Figure 4.9 (page 58). Master Quan taught that all other mantras operate through this root mantra. For some patients, he would only use the meditation mudra to move healing qi, light, and information. He explained that sometimes the root meditation mudra proved more effective because it created less conflict with their beliefs. Importantly, he was able to accomplish the same result either by using specific mudras or the root meditation mudra. The essential insight is that when you practice Spiral Dragon Meditation, this single mudra can integrate all your experiences and awareness holistically. Nonetheless, you will still find other mudras useful for specific applications and later higher-level practices.

There are mudra systems that present many variations on hand and finger correspondences to the five elements, planets, mantra syllables, colors, and chakras. Each system of spiritual practice, with its differing sets of correspondences, has been observed and designed to support that particular practice tradition. As presented in Table 8.1 below, one is not better than another. However, it is best to use a system consistent with your practice so it does develop synergy with momentum. It is also fine to examine, test, and experiment with the different systems if you are seeking greater and more comprehensive wisdom. Please refer to Table 8.1 on page 105 for a shorthand view of mudra hand and finger correspondences. To discover how Master Quan's mudra system of fingers correspond to the chakras, place your palms over your navel. The natural order of your fingers there shows the connection. Your little finger indicates its correspondence to the root or first chakra while ascending fingers show the correspondences from second up to the fifth chakra.

You will find variability in the Yoga schools interchanging the ring finger as connecting to Earth and the little finger connecting to water. You will also find minor differences in planetary correspondences to the fingers as well in different astrology systems. Whether we consider elements, colors, planets, mantras, devas, Buddhas, or any of a host of other interconnected qualities, they all vary. Try not to engage the logical assumption that one of them is correct and the rest are not. These systems of correspondences support lower or higher levels of integrated inner cultivation and as such are all true. The question is whether the system is compatible with your spiritual practice path at the moment. Perhaps a more visceral indicator are your direct perceptions arising from a meditative state of not analyzing and thinking. Which colors, chakras, and elements do you directly perceive connect to your hand and fingers? That information is more valuable for you.

TABLE 8.1. COMPARING CORRESPONDENCES IN MUDRA SYSTEMS

Digit	Yoga	Kriya	Dzogchen Kalachakra*	Kalachakra	Master Quan
Thumb	Fire	Sun	Guru	Yellow/Earth	Fifth Chakra/Space
Index	Air	Jupiter	Vajra	White/Water	Fourth Chakra/Air
Middle	Space	Saturn	HUNG	Red/Fire	Third Chakra/Fire
Ring	Earth	Venus	Padma	Black/Air	Second Chakra/Water
Pinkie	Water	Mercury	Siddhi	Green/Space	First Chakra/Earth
Palm	N/A	Mars	AUM	N/A	N/A

*This system of Dzogchen Kalachakra connects the syllables of Padmasambhava's mantra to fingers and palms. This correspondence system comes from a terma of Padma Drangnag Lingpa, as taught by Khenchen Lama Rinpoche.[1]

Fields of Sense Information

Although many people have visual impressions, or hear unheard sounds, the senses of touch, smell, and taste may be more developed in you. Schemes of mystic correspondences less often systematically correlate information from the three other senses. When it comes to mudras or movements, you have to investigate on your terms. Make your own experiments and learn what each finger represents per your own discoveries. If you perceive consistent color impressions that is your data, but equally you may smell different flowers or foods consistently as you explore what lies unlocked in your palms and fingers. Don't paint yourself into the box of making yourself an information specialist in one or two senses. Allow all your impressions to connect with wisdom. Let your learning be spontaneous, while also checking the connections to your palms and fingers over time, looking for consistent versus changing patterns. Open, test, and trust your own perceptions.

Whole Hand Spiral Dragon Mudras

I want to present a few whole hand mudras that work in adaptations of basic Spiral Dragon exercises. You may have already figured out some of these mudras, but I want to add a few more practical words with pictures. These all work more effectively after performing Relax and Sky Dragon exercises as they will intensify both your energy and awareness and the echoes and imprints of anything in your environment that you choose to explore.

Exercise

CONTACTING AND INTENSIFYING

1. Before making a connection with an Earth energy or intelligence like a particular feature of a mountain, do a Zen bow called *gassho*.* Then ask permission to learn something that will help you and others as well.
2. Once you have received assent to continue, make the intention to learn. Be more specific in asking what you want to know. Then, completely release your intention.
3. Next, intensify your connection with something near or far but within your field of vision. After you are able to do this with something you can see,

---

**Gassho* means to place your palms together at the heart. The practice originated in India and is used to greet a person reverently while saying *namaste*. On a conventional level, *gassho* means *hello*, *goodbye*, or *thank you*. In Zen, a *gassho* is accompanied by a silent, slight bow to express deep gratitude, honor, and connection.

you can extend your connection to exploring an object much farther away, or just out of sight, like on the far side of a building blocking your direct view.
4. Rotate your hands inward in the Spiral Dragon Hands posture which is aimed at a forty-five-degree angle into the Earth. See Figure 4.1 (page 47) to confirm your posture.
5. Elevate your hands to the level of your heart and face the object with which you wish to connect. Align your view and hands with the object you are investigating. Hold this posture for several periods of a twenty-one count, remembering to relax in between.
6. Move your palms so your fingers point upward, but continue to hold your arms chest high. See Figure 8.1 below. Pulse energy, alternating pushing and pulling energy toward you in sets of twenty-one counts. Remain

Fig. 8.1. Posture connecting to and concentrating energy and information from unseen distant sources.
Photo by Kaleigh Brown.

relaxed because in the Spiral Dragon connection state, you will integrate more easily and thoroughly. Practice as long as you are relaxed and are receiving impressions and information.

7. You can do this same exercise when you aim to connect with the sun, moon, stars, cloud formations, or other weather or sky phenomena.

On some occasions, like being at a sacred place, you may want more personal guidance or information to resolve a problem, but you don't have a singular question. There are two different Spiral Dragon exercises you might try. The first is pulsing the Earth as described in chapter seven (see page 95). The second exercise is to sit or stand placing your hands as shown below in Figure 8.2.

Fig. 8.2. Posture passively receiving energy and information with one hand.
Photo by Kaleigh Brown.

Exercise

RECEIVING ENERGY AND INFORMATION PASSIVELY

1. Raise your left hand so it faces outward at shoulder level while holding your right hand in half of the meditation mudra just under your navel. The purpose of holding your right hand at the navel in this position is to protect your energy so you can receive a clearer signal.
2. Focus your attention in the palm of your left hand, but place your mind in meditative awareness.
3. Like tuning a radio dial to receive a stronger signal, you can shift where you aim your left hand.
4. Hold this posture in as relaxed a manner as possible, absorbing energy and information until you sense completion.
5. At the conclusion, contemplate and record your impressions. You can be brief.

This same technique works when you do have a specific target, like the eye of the dragon feature on a distant mountain. You may not know the exact question to ask, but you recognize that you can learn something important for yourself or others. Because Spiral Dragon is a practice that transcends local space and time conditions, you do not need to be physically at a place from which you would like to receive energy or information. Master Quan often sought and received guidance from Mount Kailash, the sacred mountain of many Indian, Tibetan, and Asian spiritual traditions.

You may also send energy or information to support, heal, or connect with another person or place. The posture is a reversal of the last one discussed and is shown and described on page 110 in Figure 8.3.

Exercise

SENDING ENERGY AND INFORMATION

1. Place your right hand at shoulder height facing outward. You will send energy outward to your visible or invisible target with this hand.
2. Place your left hand in the meditative mudra just below your navel. This will protect your energy field as well as help you circulate the flow of information harmoniously.
3. Make the intention of information or energy you want to send, and the place or person whom you intend to receive it.
4. Place your attention on your right palm. You can push and pull energy with that hand to help you connect and send. Maintain meditative awareness until you sense you have transmitted what you intend to send.

Fig. 8.3. Posture sending energy and information with one hand.
Photo by Kaleigh Brown.

Pay attention to the dynamism of your own experience. If it contradicts any theoretical framework you believe, don't discard your present awareness offhand. Also remember that you will need to explore any awareness that contradicts your expectations with patience and thoroughness. The path of Spiral Dragon that accelerates performance of your personal dharma and destiny has to open new horizons, skills, and knowledge that are as yet not completely known to you nor to the world at large.

One more mudra to accelerate your progress is below in Figure 8.4. Although the thumbs-up sign is common in our worldwide culture to indicate that everything is good, or give the signal to go ahead, if you look at the thumb another way, it also appears as a flame, while the hand and fingers act as the lamp base serving as a vessel for the universal fuel of energy. This mudra expresses life force as fire, not a flickering flame, but as a strong, stable, and fiery presence. Master Quan liked that this mudra had two positive meanings: thumbs-up and life force. Usually, we make this gesture for a few seconds, but instead, try holding it for a few minutes with your left hand in the half-meditation mudra and right hand in the life torch mudra as shown below. This mudra connects to and increases the long-life energy flow of the Blue Beryl Medicine Buddha.

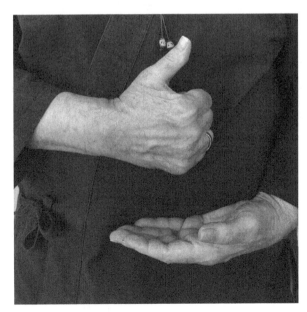

Fig. 8.4. Life Torch enlightenment flame mudra with both hands.
Photo by Kaleigh Brown.

Mantra
Resonating with Geometries of Sound

Tibetan Buddhist tantra uses the phrase "body, speech,* and mind" to refer to the interconnected trio of body, breath, and mind. Each of the similar terms, *breath*, *speech*, and *voice*, points out a different aspect of qi that resonates and moves with sound energy. The very basis for Spiral Dragon relaxation is accomplished by making an internal **HA** sound which releases stress and blockages and thereby opens the meridians to revert to the dynamics of primordial flow. Also, as you know, Master Quan prescribed very particular mantra recitations as described in chapter five to overcome obstacles during practice in the example of how to deal with sudden depletion. Mantras and Spiral Dragon together, create a synergy to dissolve obstructions as you uncover them. This is true of mudras and Spiral Dragon as well. For the rest of this chapter, we will consider all three (Spiral Dragon, mantra, and mudra) as complementary and a complete dharma system.

> Audio recordings of these mantras can be found at
> https://audio.innertraditions.com/spiraldragondharmagate/

The most common reaction to a suggestion to chant a given mantra is: What does it mean? Although that can be answered approximately, and not often satisfactorily, the more important underlying question is: What does this mantra do? The primal level of mantra is sound vibration. As you voice it, your body, energy meridians, chakras, and awareness selectively resonate in harmony. The purpose of mantra is to use this mind tool to adjust your imbalances on a vibratory level. Mantra chanting can even move beyond your body limits to synchronize the frequency of your vibration with the geography and ecology of your local environment. It is remarkably powerful.

How to Practice Mantra

Let us focus first on the **HA** mantra that is pivotal in the initial Relax exercise, but extends through all Spiral Dragon exercises. **HA** can be

---
*Sometimes *voice* or *energy* is translated in place of *speech*.

voiced at three levels. The first is to say it out loud, whether sung or spoken loudly or in a normal, conversational tone. Language and sounds of all types at this level primarily resonate with the body and physical world. While practicing, you could project the **HA** sound very audibly. Sometimes you say this automatically as when you step into bath water that is too hot for you. Usually, **AH** or **HA** comes out unthinkingly just to adjust our condition to the environment. If the water is hot, but within tolerance, you might continue to say **AHH, AAH, HAA, AHH, AHH**, automatically elongating the sounds you make as you slowly submerge yourself in the bath. During the voicing, you are relaxing into the ambient water. Similarly, during Spiral Dragon you may spontaneously and audibly breathe **HA** out. It will help your body relax. The practice instructions, however, are to say **HA** at the level of a hum, so that only you or someone very close to you are able to hear. More importantly, feel the vibration energize you. This intoning of **HA**, or any mantra, operates at the physical and energy levels. An even subtler activation of **HA** occurs when you think it without voicing it so that it operates at the mind level. In the beginning stages of your practice, stick to making a barely audible sound vibration. Later on, please experiment with each of these three levels of mantra and confirm for yourself what arises in your experience.

Master Quan made a deep study and practice of mantras and sound for inner transformation. Here, I will present but a few insights he shared that will inspire your own study and practice of mantra. One type of mantra is a natural mantra, like **AUM** and **HA** and his mantras for wellness and qi retrieval. They derive more from the science of sound and its subtler effects on our bodies, energies, and awareness. These do not originate exclusively from any spiritual tradition, but there is overlap among spiritual traditions about aspects of mantra as they arise from dharma, or natural, universal truth. One insight Master Quan taught that I had not heard before is the influence of geography on how a person hears sound and is able to replicate that sound with her or his own voice. As an example, consider how the original mantra of Amitabha Buddha* transmitted from Sanskrit-speaking India is differently pronounced in languages from other Buddhist countries even as they seek to speak the Sanskrit sounds:

India: **AUM AMITABHA HRI!** and **NAMO AMITABHAYA BUDDHAYA!**

Tibet: **AUM AMI DEWA HSRI!**

China: **NAMO OMI TO FU!**

Japan: **NAMU AMIDA BUTSU!**

North America: **AUM OH MAY DO BU SUI!**[†]

Geography influences not only the language that people in a given region speak, but actual, common sounds, all of which filter through the telluric currents, tectonic plates and substructures, mineral composition, surface landforms, rivers, lakes, bays, peninsulas, plains, valleys, and mountains of an area. Sound waveforms are changed by the mediums through which they pass. As people attune to their environments, they resonate to the sound waveforms they feel as well. What this means is that if a people are unable to precisely pronounce a foreign mantra in the language of their homeland, it is not a fault. Rather, they are connecting to the dynamic of the living mantra in the location where they live which modifies the mantra as much as it shapes their underlying native language.

The speech sounds humans make have to do with their breath, vocal cords, and resonating chambers of chest, throat, mouth, and head. This branch of linguistics is important in exploring the range of possible human speech and sound. Sacred languages present their alphabets with vowel sounds first, then move to consonant sounds originating at the back of the throat, across the soft and hard palates, to the teeth and lips. This is exactly how Sanskrit is arranged, based on the ancient sci-

---

*Amitabha Buddha, one of the five primordial (or *dhyani*) buddhas of Mahayana Buddhism, is the Buddha of Infinite Light which is the translation of his Sanskrit name.
†Per Master Quan.

ence of speech sounds. Sanskrit as a spoken and chanted language was perfected on the principle of resonance, which became the foundation of the science of mantras. In fact, *samskrtam* means *completely made* or *perfected*. It is reverence for this sacred perfection that motivated neighboring cultures who assimilated Sanskrit mantras to pronounce them as closely as possible to transmit the same precision of sound energy. Even so, Master Quan contended it is not strict fidelity to Sanskrit that is required, but rather fidelity to allowing Earth to resonate through mantras chanted locally. Allow me to connect the instruction in the Spiral Dragon Hands exercise to pulse twenty-six kilometers deep into the Earth. The depth of the Spiral Dragon practitioner's Earth connection allows not only for the thorough purification of our qi, but allows us to engage with sound vibrations beyond human hearing as they too filter through the Earth.

Although many of the mantras flowing into America derive from various traditions of Indian spirituality expressed in Sanskrit, there are mantras that originate in other cultures and languages. The tradition of mantras even goes so far as to recognize that the words and sounds of some mantras come from unseen realms, like that of the devas, nagas, mamos, and a host of worlds of other sentient beings.* There are certain gurus that have the ability to discover mantras that are useful blessings for people living now. The Sanskrit name for these gurus is *Mantrakaras* or mantra composers. They listen, transpose, and record mantra sounds in the letters of a particular language. What they attune to are higher vibratory realms from which they retrieve songs, chants, and mantras to perform in our human realm. Both traditional and newly inspired mantras are sound scripts that we can play through our

---

*In shared Hindu and Buddhist cosmology, a great number and variety of beings exist of which humans of our day are mostly unaware. These beings are aware of humans, are more long-lived than humans, and are negatively and positively affected by humans. Among these are devas, nagas, and mamos who each inhabit their own realms that overlap the human world. They have their own languages, cultures, destinies, and mantras. Humans can connect with these beings psychically, but more reliably through mantra to increase positive connection with them.

bodies and auras. The great repetition of particular mantras prescribed by spiritual traditions is a recognition that entraining our energies to the mantra's frequency requires overwriting long-standing, usually difficult karmic tendencies present in our bodies and auras so we can alter and elevate our subtle vibrations.

An important dynamic Master Quan taught is that any given mantra has seven iterations each operating at successively higher levels of consciousness. The differences in these sets of seven mantras do not arise from geographical inflection. It is as if geography influences horizontal differences in mantras across the globe while seven levels of increasing subtlety of awareness influence vertical differences. When we consider the topic of mantras, it is in an area of intersection between Spiral Dragon, Buddhism, and other mantra traditions. Since this book is primarily about Spiral Dragon, I will give just a quick example here of one particular mantra for your contemplation. It is commonly called the Buddhist Heart Sutra mantra and includes the first three of the seven vertical levels of mantra consciousness:

Level 1: Meditative silence.
Articulated from Master Quan's practice and awareness.

Level 2: **GATE, GATE, PARAGATE, PARASAMGATE BODHI SWAHA!**
From the Sanskrit *Prajnaparamita Hridayam Sutra*.

Level 3: **GATE, GATE, POLOGATE POLO SAN GATE BODHI SWAHA!**
Articulated from Master Quan's practice and awareness.

In addition, Master Quan gave individual mantras to some students to practice to improve their health or to overcome some life obstacle. These might be an entire mantra to be recited as he instructed. He also gave mantras that were missing syllables. The entire benefit of the mantra depended on the student realizing the exact missing syllable and placing it in the correct sequence. As you practice Spiral Dragon and related mantras, you are continually refining your qi which in turn refines your perception and intelligence.

How to Practice Mantra

There are a few guides to mantra practice, the first of which is to pronounce it properly. In practice that means to pronounce the mantra as closely as possible to your guru's instructions including chanting in the same rhythm. The next guide is to chant so only you can hear the mantra. This means that you can also feel the sound vibrations with your body. You can feel your body vibrate as a whole, or if you are healing a particular area, you can especially sense the vibrations moving there. As you focus on a body part, you can experiment by widening or narrowing your focus field for healing effects. The next guide is to allow for natural spontaneity to modify both the pronunciation and rhythm of the mantra. These changes can arise for a few moments or for many minutes. When the union of energy of your body and the self-adjusting mantra resolves and releases, then return to chanting as you were originally instructed. Finally, in Spiral Dragon, there is no visualization practice connected with mantra recitation. Maintain your awareness as described in Spiral Dragon Meditation, but allow visualizations and other sensations to arise naturally. Learn from them, but allow them to dissolve as you return to primordially aware mind. This chapter on mantras and mudras will become more useful to you as your experience deepens. To conclude this discussion of mantras and Spiral Dragon, I refer you to Appendix 1 which is a compilation of Master Quan's mantras and pronunciation instructions. Extra mantras are included there having to do with planetary topics of easing earthquakes and ameliorating eclipse stress.

9
Infinite Light Path of Bodhi Mind

Exploring the Limits of Intention

One day, my discussion with Master Quan turned to the subject of black magic, which arose naturally from the case of one of his patients. A very skilled black magician had been draining this patient's energy for many years since she was young. Master Quan taught me a mantra to repel this type of energy, but said that his healing strategy in this case was to pull back all the energy stolen by this black magician and return it immediately to his patient and to everyone else who was also affected. The black magician was a prominent religious figure who had betrayed his position of trust and had actively been drawing and draining life force from many thousands of people over the course of his life. In the moment Master Quan returned all the stolen life force energies, the force of negative karma also was released back upon the black magician. In instant retaliation to what had just happened, the black magician appeared as a fierce astral, green dragon looking to utterly destroy Master Quan and his intervention. Master Quan repulsed the retaliation attempt and the patient's health and life force did improve remarkably after that. However, I had more questions for Master Quan.

Obviously, the black magician was powerful and skilled, so how had Master Quan been able to subdue him so deftly? He reflected that realizing two qualities of consciousness allow him to subdue any enemy of dharma. The first is infinite intention integrated with the second, complete bodhi mind. "As long as I project no specific, personal intention, no one with a trace of self-interest can overcome that. There is nothing for another to attach to and nothing to confront in the face of limitless compassion." He went on to explain that this is true for any dharma practitioner with complete bodhi mind because any action you take arises with the force of infinite compassion. The action does not arise from the false knot of an illusory self, but from the whole field of energy, wisdom, and compassion of all the awakened ones, Buddhas and Bodhisattvas. Objectively, intention and compassion seem different, but when acting from the enlightened, bodhi mind, they arise inseparably and spontaneously as one.

We need to consider this discussion because it presents an underlying, frustrating paradox about playing with intention and motivation in Spiral Dragon. There are both philosophic and practical solutions to this paradox, but in keeping with Master Quan's approach, we will explore the direct, practical aspect. When you first start Spiral Dragon, you may interpret the Relax exercise to be primarily about letting go of tensions that constrict your body. If you only direct relaxation at that level, you gloss over dissolving harassing thoughts, afflictive emotions, and ultimately the ego complex. Any skills or improvements resulting from superficial Spiral Dragon can become an ego ornament preventing you from activating your dharma and destiny completely. Since none of us know how long it will take to engage awakened intention and bodhi mind fully, we shouldn't imagine how many gradual steps might be necessary. We need to enjoy each practice session in one-hundred-percent spontaneous presence of Spiral Dragon energy and mind. Being present in this way is the union of limitless intention and bodhi mind for that moment. Keep connecting these moments.

Master Quan used the Sanskrit *bodhicitta*, which translated in

Chinese is *pu² ti² xin¹* (菩提心), and then used the English hybrid, *bodhi mind*. For those familiar with Buddhism, bodhichitta/bodhi mind or altruistic motivation is not only a cardinal virtue, more importantly it shows where the dividing line of self-first behavior begins and ends. Greater realms of possibilities exist outside the self-imposed smaller sphere of self-interests. As long as we hold on to the perspective that *I am practicing*, or *I am progressing*, then we have established an illusory limit to what practice and progress can accomplish. Effectively, the ego just put itself in charge in order to control the flow of what is possible. Whether we establish infinite compassion as our operating platform, allow it inconsistently, or completely ignore it determines which of three different Spiral Dragon trajectories we engage.

Yoga of fire and other higher-level energy body practices draw in great amounts of qi, even though they use different transformational systems. As this great energy flows through, practitioners respond uniquely. When thoughts fluctuate a lot, first energy absorbs to balance the physical and emotional complexes* before the remaining energy is channeled to cope with life's daily challenges. When we are not overwhelmed, we can channel this extra energy influx to other uses, for example to help others. Another way to handle this energy is to try to store and amass it for other purposes, some negative, some neutral, and some well-intentioned. But in any of these approaches, life force energy can become a commodity to amass and spend strategically. The ego then seizes upon how to own, increase, and control this resource. The problem for the dharma practitioner is to be generous continuously with their qi as well as their time, effort, and physical possessions. Bodhi mind often gets subverted at this juncture because of the concern that limitless compassion will only diminish the assets the small self has at its disposal. Once

---

*Systems of the yoga of fire classify human complexes using the terms *koshas* (sheaths) and *shariras* (bodies) in Sanskrit. These are gross to super-subtle layer structures that comprise and function in embodied humans.

you begin practicing Spiral Dragon with this guarded mindset, you have entered the maze of operating a closed attitude within Spiral Dragon, an infinitely open system. Eventually, the paradox of this approach implodes, but it is possible to change to make the correct effort.

Developing limitless compassion is also a paradoxical practice. How does anyone become gradually more caring when complete transformation requires passing through the gate of active, infinite compassion? The approach is to work through the relative stages of increasing both compassionate awareness of the plight of others: humans, aliens, angels, demons, animals, plants, Earth—any being that is sentient. Compassion manifests as a visceral response to want to reduce the sufferings of sentient others, however and wherever you encounter them. When the response for others is identical to that of a parent who when caring for their own, suffering offspring jumps to immediate aid, that is compassion acting as bodhi mind.

Eight-Word Core Dharma

Some of Master Quan's students asked for a more comprehensive guide to how they should conduct their lives compassionately while practicing Spiral Dragon. In response, he presented Spiral Dragon within the context of the Buddhist path to further accelerate us to realize enlightenment and maintain a fully compassionate presence in the world. Master Quan articulated the essence of practice in an easy-to-remember scheme he referred to as the eight-word core dharma:

> *regret misdeeds,*
> *transform inside,*
> *do good,*
> *transfer merit.*

Each of these terms is a translation from Chinese into English and fails to capture the original power of the terse verse expressed. As we consider each of these individually, more of their original intent will become clear.

Regret Misdeeds

For an early translation, Master Quan chose *repent misdeeds* as repent is commonly used in Western religious practice. Connotations of *repent* are layered in centuries-old reliance on divine and institutional authorities, de-emphasizing our own continuous role and initiative in acting with compassion. *Regret misdeeds* goes more directly to the point of examining our thoughts, intentions, and actions each day from the perspective of others. How may we have injured others purposefully or inadvertently? Experiencing their pain, we should regret any negativity we have caused others, then follow it by heartfelt resolve to act positively always. The examination of our behaviors should not only include how we have impacted humans, but how we have affected sentient beings in the visible and invisible worlds. We need to correct any errors we've made immediately. If there is some injurious act which requires a sincere apology or amendment, we should set it right quickly. If it cannot be repaired directly now, we need to watch when we can take action to restore balance in the future.

This self-examination extends to looking at how we may have mistrusted our own intuition when it provided true guidance and would have created benefit for others. To develop thorough compassion, we need to amend our life course, often adjusting between unskilled actions done and good actions that were not taken but were within our power to do. Expressed positively, this advice means to be ever open and appreciative. We need to speak and act naturally with warmth, honesty, trust, integrity, fairness, and considerate directness. Our compassionate intent is to interact with an open mind to transform the mistakes we and others have made into more mutually positive outcomes. This is how to develop gradually the infinite skill of compassion despite its absolute presence in our mind stream.

Transform Inside

Nei⁴ dan¹ shu⁴ (內 丹 術) or more simply, *neidan*, is the Chinese term for a wide category of inner transformational practices that have been translated into English most often as arts of self-cultivation. *Nei* and *shu* are straightforward and mean *inner* and *art* respectively. *Dan* is more difficult because it commonly means red, vermillion, or crimson, the color of cinnabar. *Dan* also refers directly to cinnabar, the ore of mercury sulfide (chemical symbol HgS), and by extension to the use of that toxic mineral in Daoist alchemy to create an elixir to transform the human body/mind complex. We could translate *neidan* as inner alchemy, secret elixir, or inner transformation, which are the next two words of the eight-word dharma.

Transform inside is about recognizing our original nature directly and spontaneously. If we instantly recognize it, and that recognition doesn't fluctuate or glimmer away, then there is no need to do any of the practices in this category to stabilize our inherent capacity. If not, there are a vast array of mind recognition practices that we need to use to sharpen and maintain continuous recognition. Not recognizing the true nature of mind is the definition of ignorance from the Buddhist viewpoint. Inner transformation practices overcome ignorance and include practices such as Spiral Dragon, meditation, mantra, mudra, yoga, study of philosophy, healing, adopting a nurturing lifestyle, and many others. Inner transformation is an art when done with the intention to discover, express, and maintain primordial awareness. Those art forms, like martial arts or poetry, when taught with that intention are known as different types of Dao or Ways. An activity like sweeping a sidewalk is a practice from this category if the intention is to clear away your limiting perceptions as well as sweeping away the dust and oak leaves underfoot.

The category of inner transformation is not a usual description in the West for practices that refine the natural clarity of the senses and mind. There are traditional, millennia-old practices that work very well, and new ones arising to dharma practitioners on the same path to enlightenment as you. As you engage in any of these practices, you will find ones that do not help you much because you have already realized a particular level of mind-recognition. Other practices that will clarify confusion about your primordial nature are better for you out of the 84,000 possible methods and paths. And of course, a particular outward practice like a mantra can be practiced on at least seven levels of awareness, so sometimes you may only need to shift how you engage a practice to open your heart and mind.*

Do Good

The third, broad dharma practice encompasses a virtue important for most ethical and religious systems. It is to strive as often as possible to act for the best interests of others. At the very least we intend to act so as not to harm others or diminish their interests especially when our own benefit is entangled in theirs. We are to perform these good deeds for the benefit of all living beings, not only humans and animals, but also including the Earth itself, even the atmosphere encircling the planet. Our concern for others needs to grow so that we will forget ourselves in the process of caring for them. This practice unites the wisdom we have cultivated in spiritual practice with compassion in caring for all beings. At a great turning point, we actually experience that helping others is the highest form of happiness because how can we be truly happy when we participate even indirectly in the misery and suffering of others everywhere around us?

Doing good also encompasses the wisdom of when not to act in complicated circumstances without careful consideration first. One

---

*Master Quan provided a few examples of mantras that integrate each of the seven levels of consciousness. Each mantra, for instance that of Guan Yin/Chenrezig, has seven different iterations, each of which engages a corresponding level of each of the seven subtle levels of conscious awareness. I was not aware that he gave any mantra to all students or disciples as a group that was fourth level or above, but he may have done so individually. Master Quan did not define the levels of consciousness, nor how mantras operate at each level. He made it clear that when a student is ready, the next level mantra will appear in her or his mind stream.

aspect of forgetting yourself is to apply loving patience of Bodhi mind in all dealings with others. This also includes patiently allowing others ample opportunity to amend their negative behaviors. It doesn't mean accepting their indefinite negativity in harming others, but we need to allow them the chance to act compassionately. Our considered patience, however, also allows us the chance to intervene skillfully and kindly when an auspicious moment arises. Another instance of positive nonaction is not directly acting against our own interests or those who depend upon us in order to benefit others. We may not have the skill or resources available to succeed in helping another. If we are likely to injure ourselves seriously, or put our dependents at risk of harm in the effort, wisdom demands that we act instead to protect. Compassionate action requires us to recognize and avoid excessive danger. Wisdom and compassion are necessary for skillful action, and we should engage both whenever we act.

Transfer Merit

Transferring merit is about the intention and ability to release others from difficult karmas they have accumulated as suffering in body, heart, or mind. It is about transferring some of the momentum we have gained because of our dharma practice to dissolve a portion of the specific karmas of others. A practical example is that we have the ability to donate money or resources to someone in need who is in financial difficulties that they are unable to resolve themselves. Transferring our tangible resources physically to help others, however, falls more into the category of doing good. Transferring merit in Buddhism and other traditions is a much more subtle act of generosity from an advanced yogi to someone struggling in need. For an act of pure generosity, you directly do good with no need to understand another's karma in order to benefit them. To transfer merit, your skill and awareness need to be much greater.

Karma is the accumulation of what we have created by our thoughts, words, and deeds since beginningless time. It is like layers of clouds over the sun that cover the view of original nature. Karma presents an illusion which we mistakenly assert as absolutely true. It operates to magnetize experiences that confirm the familiar illusions we perceive as real. Enlightened mind exists beyond the wheel of time while the realm of karma operates completely within the wheel of time. In order to transfer merit, we have to be able to see the world of karma relatively, as it operates according to the laws of cause and effect, and yet maintain the view of enlightenment from outside of time. While perceiving both aspects, we will know how to untangle the karma of others at a profoundly effective level so they awaken to enlightenment. Within the Sanskrit-speaking spiritual traditions of India, great practitioners have been called mahatmas (great souls), siddhas (perfected ones), mahasiddhas (great perfected ones), gurus, mahagurus (great gurus), as well as many other honorifics. The main siddhi (perfection) they display is enlightenment, but they also display lesser spiritual powers such as the ability to transfer merit to dissolve karma.

To approach transferring merit from a more practical side, let us consider the art of healing to enter the field of this siddhi and approach its center. Though there are many healing methods, here we consider what we discussed previously as adjuncts of Spiral Dragon: qi healing, mantra recitation, and mudras. Starting with energy healing there are many variants, but where we leave the tangible healing of the body is when we heal others with directed qi flow. At first, we may direct qi, amplified by mantra recitation, to a certain area to affect the physical body. Later, as with acupuncture and *kiatsu** therapies, we may direct qi quite specifically to balance a patient's own qi flow. We may intervene at progressively more subtle structures like bindus (energy nodes), chakras, koshas, shariras, or far beyond what we can catalog. Early in this book, we discussed stages of Spiral Dragon of qi transforming into light, and light eventually transforming into limitless information. Qi

---

*Kiatsu is a form of healing that combines and infuses *ki* (the Japanese equivalent of qi) with shiatsu therapy.

healing is an example of initiating the transfer of merit. Depending on the Spiral Dragon practitioner's realization and skill, qi healing eventually will be healing through light.

Recall that once we place ourselves in the dynamic and open energy of Spiral Dragon, we are outside local time/space containment and therefore partially outside local karma. We may not know the coordinates of where we are in time and space, but we have shifted our own karma so that to some degree we are operating from the threshold of enlightenment. From that awareness in cosmic presence, we can experiment with transferring merit and learn what we can accomplish to help others. In teaching about transfer of merit in tandem with Spiral Dragon, Master Quan affirmed our ability to connect and operate at this high level. Spiral Dragon can facilitate the accelerated development of our unique dharma in this crucial time. It also facilitates the ability to share our unique skills and attainments to benefit many others, practically and karmically. Spiral Dragon is a direct doorway to developing the siddhi of transferring merit, of sending awakened light across time and space to relieve suffering and assure the well-being of sentient beings in all circumstances and places.

Master Quan asked his students to apply the eight-word core dharma continuously to review our own efforts and to enlighten our hearts and mind. Thereby, we can transform all our likes and dislikes into a fount of benefit for all sentient beings. The eight-word dharma presents Spiral Dragon within a larger context, but it also suggests a synergy of enlightenment practices assuring us that our efforts are magnified in the right direction.

Signs of Regress and Progress

I would like to conclude this book by briefly presenting some guidance on signs that show that you are continuing to engage Spiral Dragon productively. What narrows Spiral Dragon dynamic down the most is selfish intentionality, whether engaging in intense black magic, or telling yourself white lies that you will help others at some distant date.

Self-first goals will weigh you down as your body will feel denser and heavier, your emotional attachments will increase in number and intensity, and your mind will fixate in obsessive circles. Mostly, you will not experience much positive change in your life from this type of practice irrespective of your efforts. However, if you feel that your body, emotions, and life worries become lighter when you engage in Spiral Dragon, that is a very positive sign. This results in experiencing happiness as you are able to let go of the burdens and limits you carry. The more you play openly with Spiral Dragon, the more difficulties you will be able to surrender to the cosmos.

Sometimes self-involvement can be subtle and sensual. Master Quan had several Spiral Dragon students in Shanghai who experienced frequent involuntary movements that would seize them at inconvenient moments, day or night. Sudden fits would arise whenever they began doing the third exercise, Spiral Dragon Hands. They would push and pull energy starting abruptly, continuing for a time, then stopping inexplicably as if they were puppets. There was nothing they could do to control the onset or end, so they asked Master Quan for advice. His assessment was that their intention for practicing Spiral Dragon was because they were greedy for qi, its sensation, flow, and power. The students previously had practiced qi gong, but switched to Spiral Dragon when the results they wanted came more quickly and palpably. Their obsession with qi, however, produced an unexpected obstacle that could have ended if they had been able to let go of their greed for qi.

Signs of negative practice arise when we practice without depth of engagement, not momentarily, but day after day. This includes not taking time to relax, having specific and strong expectations, and competitively driving ourselves toward visible outward accomplishments. When we start training ourselves like Olympic-aspiring athletes, we are on the wrong track. At each moment of practice something valuable is revealed, meant especially for us to resolve our life impasses. When we are so obsessed with achieving some result that we pay little attention to present revelations, we waste much of our efforts and guidance.

Positive signs appear when we become aware that we are radiating the Spiral Dragon dynamic especially outside a practice session. I've described this experience earlier, but want to re-emphasize its importance as it is easy to overlook. When any of the sensations from Sky Dragon appear spontaneously while engaged in your daily regimen, that is a moment to recognize and savor. The experience of Relax and Sky Dragon, amplified by the three energy-moving exercises, will manifest in unique ways that are particular to you. Among the signs are feeling energy indirectly so that:

1. Your body may sway gently.
2. Your palms may become redder, tingle, or have light blotches.
3. Your palms or body may feel warmer irrespective of outside temperature.
4. Your feet may feel as if they are connected and open to the Earth.
5. You may often forget your self-identity and simply feel happy.
6. You may have a heightened sense of nature's energies around you.
7. You may feel comfortably centered at your navel, heart, or third-eye chakras.
8. You often experience moments of incredible insight and inspiration.

The more often these sensations manifest naturally, the more positive is the sign that you are present in the Spiral Dragon dynamic that is at the root of consciousness. The foregoing signs often appear in concert with deep contentment and happiness in the present. They appear as you recognize an increase in your intelligence arising as a string of *ah-ha* moments. These frequent awakenings interconnect your experience and learning in new and surprising ways that prove true. These signs of accomplishment especially appear when you encounter a person who is struggling and, without reservation, you are immediately moved to relieve their suffering if you can. In addition to feeling wider and deeper compassion, another important sign of accomplishment is both feeling and recognizing that you are living frequently in a state of inspiration, creativity, and freedom of unlimited horizons.

Hands and Enlightenment

As discussed earlier, hands are essential to the play and practice of Spiral Dragon. The evolution of the hominid hand expressing prehensible and opposable thumbs created a distinguishing characteristic in humans increasing the range of hand functions, manual dexterity, and fine motor skills all particular to humans. Various human species evolved physical hand capabilities from *homo habilis* through *homo sapiens*, thereby accelerating the creation and refinement of hand tools and hand technologies. Hands show up all around the world in the petroglyphs and pictographs of many ancient peoples who celebrate the importance and sacred power of hands. These ubiquitous art themes reveal human hands as gates opening the depths of the universe. See Figure 9.1 below.

Fig. 9.1. Hand pictographs as archetypal art themes from Cueva de Las Manos, Santa Cruz Province, Patagonia, Argentina, circa 5,000 BCE.

Infinite Light Path of Bodhi Mind ∞ 131

Fig. 9.2. Statue of the Medicine Buddha with right hand in the mudra of generosity revealing a diamond in the palm as a mark of complete enlightenment.

132   Infinite Light Path of Bodhi Mind

Fig. 9.3. Close-up of the Medicine Buddha's diamond palm of enlightenment.

In Spiral Dragon we recognize the energetic importance of hands. In Korean Koryo traditional medicine, hands are a special microsystem with the capability to raise us above to our highest wellness level in this life. Every Spiral Dragon exercise relies on the inherent ability of our hands to orchestrate increased and balanced qi. With greater refinement, Spiral Dragon mudras extend our skills and awareness of how to help others by magnifying and sharing energy. Exploring new ways to transmit qi though your hands and apply that knowledge to your life skills creates the ability to accelerate your own life dharma/destiny to bring greater worldwide benefit at this crux of human history.

Finally, and most importantly, our hands display our Spiral Dragon state. In the long term, our hands also display progress to enlightenment, especially in the palm lines that change with continued practice. Examine the subtle changes to the lines in your palms both left and right regularly. It reveals karma you are changing, whether dissolving difficult karmas, or creating and enhancing beneficial karmas. The ultimate sign that you are near realization of enlightenment is that a diamond will appear, composed of the lines in your palm. You were born with the first line complete, referred to as the life line in palmistry. In the course of Spiral Dragon three more lines appear and connect to produce your hand diamond. It is shown in Figures 9.2 and 9.3 which are images of the Medicine Buddha statue from Master Quan's Life Torch Bodhi Temple.

EPILOGUE
Dharma Unfolding Destiny

Life leads the thoughtful man on a road of many windings.[1]

KONG FU ZI (CONFUCIUS)

One day, I met a person who attended a class I taught the year before. She said: "Wait a minute, I know you. You're the feng shui guy!" I nodded, because it had become part of my dharma, a completely unforeseen destiny thread. Since I had grown up with no awareness of feng shui, this new career path stands as an example of how Spiral Dragon integrated my previous learning and experience into an unfolding dharma stream without my specific intention. From the time I met Master Quan and began Spiral Dragon, my life experiences reassembled into an alternate order for a life work I had not planned, but for which I was mostly prepared. Consciously I had prepared myself to be a writer, so it was natural that I would subsequently write a few books presenting feng shui wisdom that emerged from my experiences.* Some other force above or beyond my day-to-day awareness was and has been guiding my path. As our compassion grows, some higher order reassembles our skills and knowledge into ever higher order dharmas. Looking back, I see how feng shui has allowed me to open and engage more deeply with sacred places. Preeminent among sacred places is the realm of Shambhala.

---

*These two books are *Feng Shui: Art and Harmony of Place* and *Realty Feng Shui: Places and Profits in the Marketplace.*

I have had an interest in Shambhala ever since my mother took me to the Shangri-La Chinese restaurant in Chicago's Loop. Forty years later, I was seated at a Chinese restaurant in Lhasa at the base of the Potala Palace, the winter palace of the Dalai Lama. I was with Master Quan and students, seated with the best view of the white and red palace rising above. I really couldn't manage to eat much as I was overcome with intensity. My feeling was not nostalgic longing for the past, but more a sense of familiar recognition that I had seen this view frequently before. No one else at the table seemed as awestruck. If ever a place appeared as the setting for a past life, the Potala Palace was one of the most powerful I encountered.

In 2016, Hapi Hara and I began a series of public presentations exploring the feng shui of sacred places and their connection to crystals and the *chintamani*, the wish-fulfilling mind gem. This collaboration led to our book, *The Chintamani Crystal Matrix: Quantum Intention and the Wish-Fulfilling Gem*. We were led to revelations of how sacred places, gems, and the science of intentionality were entwined with the chintamani, Shambhala, and the awakening mind. As research unfolded, we studied guide books by Tibetan tantric gurus and masters that describe how to find Shambhala on the search through dimensions of mind and place. The Spiral Dragon pilgrimage with Master Quan was my formal initiation to search seriously for Shambhala. The guidebooks direct the quest to begin in Lhasa, the place of gods.*

The Potala Palace is a remarkable building incorporating sacred geometry, superlative feng shui, and centuries of continuous tantric ritual practices on and under Ri Marpo, the Red Mountain. It was built in two

---

*Many cultures, philosophies, and religions refer to a realm similar to Shambhala, the place of peace. Shambhala in the traditions of India is a place well-hidden from the general public led by a council of realized sages who guide the physical, cultural, and spiritual development of the world. Buddhist Shambhala is a place where the Kalachakra tantra, an extensive set of outer, inner, and secret yogas, continues to be taught and practiced by its inhabitants. Shambhala in the Indian traditions is the kingdom that will defeat power-hungry rulers and inaugurate a golden age of worldwide peace and enlightenment.

phases, the first by King Songsten Gampo and his Tang dynasty consort, Princess Wenchang, in the seventh century. A thousand years later, it was substantially reconstructed by the Fifth Dalai Lama to manifest the Bodhisattva Chenrezig, and reconstitute the seat of Tibetan government. I toured the Potala with Master Quan, with whom I visited some of its many chapels and viewed collections of thangkas and art on display. We encountered an amazing mandala, perhaps six feet square by four feet high, constructed of thousands of pearls. Pearls are one of the gems from Chinese and Tibetan learning identifiedas the chintamani. Chenrezig is often pictured holding a chintamani at his heart vowing benefit to all sentient beings. The three-dimensional pearl mandala strongly resonated Chenrezig, compassion, and the chintamani.

We stayed at a hotel close to the Potala, affording ample opportunity to sense and explore its energy field and treasures. Avalokiteshvara/Guan Yin/Chenrezig is presented in various forms and colors. There is a four-armed white Chenrezig like the color of the lower floors of the Potala, and there is a red form of Chenrezig like the name of the mountain and color of the upper floors. One night, I slipped unseen out of the hotel to explore Lhasa. I walked to the Potala without looking too out of place because there is a hotel on the grounds hosting Western visitors. I got as close as I could to the base of the daunting complex and practiced Spiral Dragon. As I looked up at the white and red palaces, seven stories above, I inquired about the future freedom of tantric Buddhism in Tibet. After connecting with the energies and intelligence present, I saw an imposing vision of a transparently orange-colored Chenrezig rising high above the building. In that visionary moment I realized Tibet and its treasures have not been lost, but we must radiate compassion to restore the great scale of its future positivity.

On our Lhasa tour, we went to the Norbulingka or Jewel Place, the summer residence of the Dalai Lamas. *Jewel* has two ready associations in this context. The first is that the Buddha, Dharma, and Sangha are invoked as the Three Jewels to guide Buddhist practitioners to enlightenment. The second is the *yishin norbu* or chintamani which serves as a guide to Shambhala. There amid eighty-nine acres of the highest cultivated garden in the world sits the Norbulingka Palace. It was here that Master Quan discussed the essence of Kalachakra teachings as the ability to move out of the causality of karma and time. He emphasized that Spiral Dragon accomplishes the Kalachakra tantra.

Master Quan performed a number of initiations for us while we were in Lhasa including the Medicine Buddha and White Tara. On the journey to Shambhala, and especially during its final stages, White Tara appears as a guide. Skilled Kalachakra yogis have reported dreams or visions of White Tara appearing as a common person at first, only later to appear in her form as a Bodhisattva. She flies the practitioner over the surrounding protective mountains on the last leg of the journey to the central palace of the capitol city, Kalapa. There, the practitioner can ask any question of the Kalachakra Master, the Kalki King, to dissolve remaining doubts and obstacles, and become clear to enter the sacred mandala's realm.

Some years later, I purchased a Kalachakra mandala* which had been painted by a master thangka painter at a Nepalese temple in accord with Tibetan tantric art tradition. The mandala has an orange background like the Chenrezig apparition I experienced in Lhasa. More importantly, it had been painted with mineral and gem pigments so that by holding my palm a foot away from the canvas, I could feel the warm and palpable minerals radiate energy and intelligence. I have practiced Spiral Dragon many times near the mandala pulsing energy back and forth to sense what I need to know. Often, I've keenly felt the presence of the awakened ones resonating the energy and consciousness of the Kalachakra teachings. Over time, Spiral Dragon play has intensified my connection through this mandala to the enlightened

---

*The Kalachakra mandala is a 2D diagram of the wheel of time. It is a map to enlightenment in the center showing the stages of how to collapse time and karma. At the outer edge are a circle of Sanskrit syllables representing the vibration of sound that is the first barrier to entry.

The Kalachakra Mandala.

beings of Shambhala and to those Bodhisattvas at work in our world who practice and transmit the path of peace and enlightenment. When times are critical, we are guided along alternate life paths to benefit the entire web of consciousness, especially now.

APPENDIX I

Spiral Dragon Mantra Wisdom

Throughout the book, we have explored Spiral Dragon together with mantras for specific purposes. Mantras allow us to achieve two types of siddhis (skill powers): supreme and mundane. The supreme siddhi is self-transformation that precipitates enlightenment. Mundane siddhis are abilities to overcome and master a range of obstacles that beset ourselves and others. Even when we are directing healing to someone, we are acting to realize our enlightenment as well as harmonizing our patient with the field of their own enlightenment. When using mantras, do have the intention for specific definable outcomes, but don't limit the mantra to produce specific effects observable by a few senses. Let your mind be completely open to allow the mantra to operate infinitely.

In this appendix you will find information assembled about how to use the mantras we've considered for easier reference. You will also find additional and related mantras with which you can experiment. The mantras considered here are both from the Sutra and Mantrayana (Tibetan Tantric) Buddhist traditions. There are also treasure contributions from Senton Dorje and Master Quan who were both Masters of the Nyingma tradition. They revealed mantras, their pronunciation, and particular uses.

Mantra Transmission and Practice Power

Mantra transmission is an energy transmission from the guru who performed an initiation or gave you instruction in how you should sound a particular mantra. This is especially true if you have received a mantra and its practice in a small group or one-on-one from a guru. If you receive a mantra from someone who hasn't practiced that mantra much or at all, it's an intellectual exchange with no dimension of energy transmission. Conversely, if you receive a mantra from a practitioner who has meditatively recited this mantra millions of times, and their teacher received it from a teacher who had also chanted it millions of times, there is a very strong energy transmission. This suggests the great value of a mantra's practice lineage.

What creates further transformative mantra power is your confidence in engaging that mantra to resolve your own karmic impasses, and to open and connect to a dynamic stream of intelligent, compassionate energy. That confidence has been called faith, reliance, or trust in the power of the mantra. It is not blind faith, but rather a trust that has proven reliable as you continue to engage and experience the mantra. This trust is more important than pronouncing the mantra perfectly, as the following story illustrates.

True Mantra Pronunciation

Master Quan relayed the traditional, tantric story of an elderly lady who practiced her mantra daily and so loudly it could be heard in the street. One day an eminent scholar monk walked by her home. He heard her mantra being horribly mispronounced and to him mis-practiced. He went to the door, and when invited in by the devout practitioner, told her how she needed to change her mantra recitation in order to be correct. After he left, she began practicing the new mantra pronunciation devoutly. A month later the scholar monk passed by the elderly lady's home and decided to stop and check how her amended practice was proceeding. She confessed to him that in her mantra chanting before, she had visions of Buddhas and Bodhisattvas and felt a constant field of compassionate and healing energy. Now, nothing like the results of her previous practice ever happened. It was correct in form, but without connection, energy, and insight. The scholar monk immediately told her to forget his instruction and return enthusiastically to her lifelong mantra practice as before. The next time the monk passed by her house some months later, he observed a dynamic display of rainbow lights extending beyond her house and into the surrounding area.

Instruction in practicing a mantra includes pronunciation, a melody if there is one, tempo, cadence, and mind state. On pronunciation, Master Quan was quite precise. Over the course of teaching mantra, he used a number of different transcription systems to convey the exact recitation sound using the English alphabet for his Western disciples and students. One convention he used that you will find below is a combination of **dT** or **pB*** to express that the pronunciation is in between voiced and unvoiced sounds. Master Quan kept tuning his hearing and chanting of new and traditional mantras to discover subtleties in sound and vibration qualities. Another spelling convention in these mantras is the underline dash. It means you should draw out the vowel sounds more slowly. The final convention I've added that Master Quan did not is the comma indicating a pause. When chanted by a group, there was usually a pause in cadence where the comma appears. There are a number of mantras in which the same sound appears, such as **AUM**, but it is not always pronounced the same way depending on the mantra in which it appears. When **AUM** appears, you blend all the letters into a sound, but not quickly. When **A_U_M** appears, lengthen the sound of each vowel but keep the sound as a continuous chant.

In chapter eight, I presented Master Quan's view of why mantra pronunciation varies from country to country in more detail. His perspective

---

***dT** indicates that the voiced **T** should be closer in sound to a **D**, while **pB** indicates that the voiced **B** should be closer in sound to a **P**.

briefly stated here and mentioned earlier in the book is that landforms in local geography cause sounds to resonate uniquely. Local residents hear and feel mantra vibrations move through their bodies as they uniquely recite what they experience. A second reason mantras vary is that any given mantra has seven potential expressions, each level differently transforming our awareness from grosser to subtler levels.

While Master Quan expected students to begin their mantra sessions with the exact instructions for chanting, he recognized that as you keep tuning into mantras, mantras in turn refine and tune you. What this means practically is that you may suddenly deviate markedly from the pronunciation, emphasis, or cadence while practicing any mantra. If this occurs spontaneously, you are in sync with the mantra. When your chanting variation stops being a spontaneous expression, return to your received mantra instructions. Variations may occur momentarily or last for longer carried by a newly arising energy of the mantra as it adjusts your body, karma, energy, or awareness. Like any yogic practice, notice when you drift away, make adjustments, then return to the heart of the practice.

Three Modes of Voicing

In chapter eight, we considered three ways to perform mantras. The first way is projecting your voice in song or audible speaking tone which emphasizes the mantra's engagement with your body and the physical world. The second way of chanting is to lower your voice to a hum so that only someone very close might be able to hear you. In this pattern you experience your own voice vibrating through your body. This mantra engagement has a greater effect on your energy field and flow. The last way of chanting is to think the mantra without hearing yourself even say these words internally. This final way places emphasis on engaging the mantra with your mind and awareness. Of course, you should experiment with the three methods to determine how they work for you. It is completely fine to alter your practice from one mode to another in the same session. As you gain more experience with mantras, you can make finer and finer adjustments to transform your condition more skillfully moment to moment.

Mantras and Visualizations

With some mantras, you are instructed to create a series of prescribed visualizations of the realms in which the mantra exists and operates. For some people, that makes mantra practice more focused and vital. Master Quan, however, instructed his students to practice any mantra with awareness only. You might focus on the sound, a point in the body/energy complex, or simply your awareness resting in the nature of mind as you chant. Mantras by themselves contain mandalas, intelligence, and connection to the minds of the awakened ones. By not imposing a preset visualization over the mantra, you allow the manifestations of the mantra to arise by themselves which may appear as colors, light radiance, specific visualizations, insight, or absorption in awareness as it is.

Mantra Repetitions

Mantras are repeated in sets of varying length, most frequently nine, twenty-one, and one-hundred eight. You have to fit your mantra practice into the time you have available. Each of these numbers is sacred. Nine is a ubiquitous, sacred number with many occult correspondences. Consider nine as being in resonance with the sun. During several total solar eclipses, Master Quan was present in the path of totality. He realized from his experiments then that the sun has nine primary rays making nine a solar number. The twenty-one repetitions mirrors twenty-one repetitions of any of the Spiral Dragon exercises and reflects the number of energy flows horizontally and vertically through the body. One-hundred eight repetitions creates a greater force because of the longer practice focus. One-hundred eight also is a sacred number that synchronizes with measures of time and space to intensify mantra practice. A few sample measures below divide evenly into one-hundred eight.

One-Hundred Eight Resonance in Time and Space

Years in the precession of the equinoxes are 25,920 = 240 x 108.

Years in a great year or age of a zodiac sign are 2,160 = 20 x 108.

Nautical miles in the circumference of Earth are 21,600 = 200 x 108.

Square inches in an acre are 6,272,640 = 58,080 x 108.

Your body proportion is 96 of your fingers high. The chakra above your head is 12 more or 108 fingers high.

Bija or Seed Syllables

Some mantras have bija or seed syllables which have greater impact than the other syllables. They are usually added at the conclusion of one-hundred-eight repetitions of a mantra as the last extra sound before beginning another set. Examples of a bija syllable added at the end are **DHI** for the Manjushri mantra and **dTAM** for the Green Tara mantra. Sometimes seed syllables are within a mantra and are voiced each time the mantra is repeated. Common seed syllables are **AUM, AH, HUNG**, and **HA**, which can be chanted alone for a set number of recitations.

Spiral Dragon Mantras for Energy and Health

The mantras presented below all create a positive synergy with Spiral Dragon for healing and regenerating your energy. They are also effective on their own. The first two are discussed in chapter six while the latter two are extra. Only the Medicine Buddha mantra is a traditional Buddhist healing mantra, whereas the others in this section were discovered by Master Quan.

The following mantra is useful when you are feeling low energy, on the verge of catching an illness, have nausea and dizziness, or are in mild discomfort or pain:

A_U_M SHA HUM ZHN CHIN OM SO HA!

If you experience sudden depletion or realize you have no energy to carry on your usual daily tasks, the next mantra is very effective. It combines chanting your name three times and then adding the mantra seven times for a total of ten repetitions per set. Repeat three, seven, fourteen, or twenty-one sets. Check to see if your energy has returned and to what degree. You only need to practice till you feel better. For your name, you can use your given name, or an initiation name you have received. Speak your name three times, then the following mantra seven times:

AUM, GA JI_U, SHU HO!

There are many cell level diseases common today, particularly cancer. The following mantra activates the cellular level of your body and repairs and re-energizes many kinds of cellular dysfunctions. You can listen to someone else chant this mantra slowly for you, but it will be much more effective for you to feel the vibrations of the sound throughout your body if you chant the mantra. It works best at a humming level of sound vibration, rather than silently chanted:

A_U_M JI_UMM SHI_UMM!

The Medicine Buddha mantra is chanted to remedy the complete range of maladies, diseases, and dysfunctions whether acute or chronic. It also begins to harmonize the underlying elemental imbalances that lead to ill health as well as resolving underlying root karmic causes of disease. Traditionally, it is chanted by healers when performing treatments on others, but is very powerful to chant when healing yourself. The first two versions are how the traditional Sanskrit and Tibetan mantras are chanted, followed by Master Quan's pronunciation:

Traditional Sanskrit: AUṂ BHAIṢAJYE BHAIṢAJYE MAHA BHAIṢAJYA RĀJA SAMUDGATE SVĀHĀ!

Tibetan pronunciation: AUṂ BEKADZE, BEKADZE, MAHA BEKADZE, RADZA SAMUDGATE SOHA!

Master Quan's version: AUM PIKADZEY, PIKADZEY, MAHAPIKADZEY, JRA ZA SAMU GATE SWA HA!

Mantras for Mothers

In Buddhism, the action of compassion compares to the natural love a mother has for her child, sacrificing her interests, even her life, for her child's benefit. The following two mantras express deep gratitude for the compassion of mothers, and also reestablishes balance and harmony when mother-child relationships were or are regrettably difficult. One mantra is for deceased mothers who are now the near line of our ancestors and integral source of half the parental DNA we carry to our heirs. These mantras recognize that despite karma seeming like a one-way path of cause and effect, as we cultivate ourselves toward enlightenment, we are liberating the whole line of our ancestors, past and future. The mantra for living mothers expresses gratitude, removes emotional barriers so we can reestablish harmonious connection, as well as heal our mothers of physical, emotional, and mental afflictions. This mantra is also very helpful in easing and strengthening difficult pregnancies that affect mother or unborn child.

For deceased mothers: **AUM AH HUNG, HU YUHOO TSEN EN DU_M SO HA!**

For living mothers: **AUM AH HUNG, HU YUHOO TSEN EN CHIN TSIN KON GA SO HA!**

Mantras for Averting Disasters and Harmonizing with Earth

Disasters, natural and devised, have been critical impediments to creating and sustaining a high culture of economic, personal, communal, artistic, and spiritual development. As a result, many prayers and mantras in every spiritual tradition are directed to uphold the collective security and well-being of society. In this section, there are mantras from Master Quan and traditional Buddhism to decrease and eliminate the negativity from various disasters. Reciting mantras inclusively for the good of all develops and expresses the compassionate ideal of Bodhichitta.

Eclipses

The first two mantras in this group are designed to reduce the negativity of solar eclipses, especially total ones. The first mantra includes your own higher-level spiritual cultivation added to the intention of decreasing negative eclipse effects before and after. If you experience any physical symptoms like headaches, undue depression, or mild heart discomforts, do this mantra immediately. The second eclipse mantra is more specifically directed to relieve damage and suffering at the physical and personal levels in the wake of a total solar eclipse, particularly along the path of totality.

AUM JU, SHU_ROO_M DU, pBENTSA!

AUM HUNG CHU, SHU-ROO-M DU, pBENTSA!

Earthquakes

This next mantra is for reducing the negative effects of earthquakes. If an earthquake is forecasted in any area on Earth, your recitation of this mantra will help reduce but not eliminate major damage. After an earthquake occurs, this mantra will improve the aid response, bringing more rapid recovery to all who are suffering.

AUM CHI-DU HONG PAY, pBA CHE DE HONG PAY,
HUNG HUNG HUNG HUNG HUNG SO HA!

Green Tara is a Bodhisattva who is renowned for her swift and compassionate intervention to reduce suffering. Tara can mean both star and protector. She is pictured sitting with her left leg in a meditative position and her right ready to step forward in immediate aid. In her mantra, the word **TURE** can mean quick action. Tara's mantra is a higher-level spiritual cultivation as well as a call for immediate help. In Tibet, Tara is invoked to reduce every type of disaster and the eight fears that attach to those common disasters including Earth disturbances, war, and epidemics.* Presented next is the traditional pronunciation compared to Master Quan's emphasis on the **T** sound as closer to the voiced **D** sound:

> Sanskrit Green Tara: **AUM TARE TUTTARE TURE SWAHA!** After one-hundred eight repetitions, add the seed syllable, **TAM.**
>
> Master Quan's Green Tara: **AUM DARE DUDDARE DURE SOHA!** After one-hundred eight repetitions, add the seed syllable, **dTANG.**

A lower-level version of the Green Tara mantra invokes immediate physical aid and removal of threats. This is the Pu Man Ping mantra. It comes from Chinese Buddhist practice, and I have not yet found this mantra paired with Green Tara in any other country's Buddhist tradition. I have used it in dire circumstances and received immediate improvements. This mantra eases emergencies, whether large-scale disasters or personal crises.

AUM DARE DARE, DUDDARE DUDDARE SO HA!

Buddhist Mantras

An incredibly large number of mantras come from Buddhism through its many sub-traditions. An extremely thorough resource for exploring Buddhist mantras in sound, image, meaning, history, and calligraphy is Jayarava's reference book, *Visible Mantra*.[1] Some mantras are completely open for anyone to recite while some tantric mantras require transmission or instruction on how to practice. The ones presented here are mantras Master Quan encouraged his disciples, Spiral Dragon

---

*The eight fears are actual external disasters, but also reflect internal negative states: (1) fear of drowning or flooding reflects craving or attachment; (2) fear of thieves reflects false perceptions; (3) fear of lions reflects pride; (4) fear of snakes reflects envy or jealousy; (5) fear of fire reflects hatred or anger; (6) fear of spirits, especially flesh-eating demons, reflects doubt; (7) fear of captivity and imprisonment reflects avarice; (8) fear of elephants reflects delusion and ignorance.

students, and their circle of family and friends to practice regularly.

Amitabha is the Buddha of Infinite Light which is the translation of his Sanskrit name. The mantra of Amitabha Buddha is a way to transform our strong desires for things, people, and events from their unsatisfactory and often painful expression into the wisdom of discriminating awareness. This mantra is also chanted for those who have recently died to open a direct path for their liberation, or at the very least ease their bardo (afterlife) passage to a better rebirth.

Traditional Tibetan version: **AUM AMI DEWA HRI!**

Master Quan's version for North America: **AUM OH MAY DO BU SUI!**

Avalokiteshvara is the Bodhisattva of infinite compassion. In India and Tibet, the male aspect of **Avalokiteshvara/Chenrezig** is popular, whereas in China, Korea, Japan, and Vietnam, the female aspect of **Guan Yin/Kannon** Bodhisattva is popular. In Sanskrit and all the translated Buddhist languages, Avalokiteshvara means *listener for the cries of suffering*. This mantra is perhaps the most well-known worldwide. Like Tara's mantra, this cry for help is swiftly answered because the Bodhisattva is actively listening and ready to put compassion in action. If you look up the meaning of the words, you may find *hail to the jewel in the lotus*. The first and last syllables, **AUM** and **HUNG**, are bija or seed syllables that activate the crown and heart chakras. **MANI PADME** means *jewel* and *lotus*. Without turning the mantra into a sentence, allow depths of meanings to arise naturally within your energy and mind.

> Sanskrit traditional mantra: **AUM MANI PADME HUNG!** After one-hundred eight repetitions, add the seed syllable, **HRI!**

> Master Quan's third level mantra: **AUM MONI POMO LOONG HUNG!** After one-hundred eight repetitions, add the seed syllable, **SUI!**

Vajrasattva Buddha's name can mean *Pristine Diamond* or *Lightning*

Being. Vajrasattva's mantra is invoked to purify yourself, food, places, or anything needing clearing from contamination whether physical, emotional, energetic, or mental. Vajrasattva has a long hundred-syllable mantra and a short six-syllable mantra presented below. Reciting Vajrasattva's mantra intensifies any physical or ritual purification you may do. Master Quan put mantras together in sequences to direct a stronger positive force. If you are reciting either or both eclipse mantras, by chanting the Vajrasattva mantra first, you will create a synergy that increases the effective force of the mantras to protect people and places from disaster.

> Traditional Sanskrit version: **AUM VAJRA SATTVA HUNG!**
>
> Master Quan version: **AUM WAJRA SATTOWA HUNG!**

Manjushri is the Bodhisattva of learning and wisdom who is shown holding a blazing sword aloft in his right hand while in his left holding a stemmed blue lotus with a book of dharma on top. The sword is the means to cut away the irrelevant to reveal the heart essence of any matter. Very commonly in Asian countries, children recite Manjushri's mantra before a written test or oral presentation so they will have greater recall and command of what they have learned. The mantra is very useful whenever we struggle to comprehend a subject or situation.

> Traditional Manjusri mantra: **AUM AH RA PA TSA NA DHI!** After one-hundred eight recitations, optionally recite the seed syllable, **DHI** one-hundred eight more times.
>
> Master Quan's version: **AUM AH RA PA TSA NA DHI DHI DHI!** This version repeats the seed syllable three times per recitation.

Vajrapani is a blue, wrathful Bodhisattva, who is pictured frequently with Avalokiteshvara and Manjusri. Together they represent different qualities needed to realize enlightened mind. Vajrapani's name means literally holder of the vajra as a diamond or as lightning. This is a wrathful mantra especially useful when you feel almost out of hope.

You may think there is not enough time to improve a crisis you are experiencing. That is exactly when you should chant this mantra with certainty to engage the enlightened power and energy necessary to help yourself and all sentient beings. This mantra also diffuses anger and aggression that you may be feeling or that is directed against you. In Tantric Buddhism, you are usually required to have Vajrapani's empowerment and instruction to use this mantra wisely. Master Quan taught it directly to disciples and practitioners without a requirement. Master Quan's and the traditional Vajrapani mantra are the same.

> **AUM VAJRAPANI HUNG!** After one-hundred eight recitations, recite the seed syllable, **PAY!**

An important mantra is from the *Prajna Paramita Hridaya Sutra*, the Heart of Wisdom Sutra. *Prajna Paramita* means the wisdom that takes you across. The mantra means *gone, gone, gone across, gone completely across*, resolving the apparent duality of all pairs of opposites in the single enlightenment of Bodhi Mind. Zen commentary on this is: "Not one, not two." This mantra is helpful in resolving impasses of opposite choices in life. It is useful when you are on the verge of transforming to a higher state of energy and awareness. The Heart Sutra mantra helps us see beyond the appearances of life to the heart essence of awareness.

> Sanskrit version: **GATE, GATE, PARAGATE, PARASAMGATE BODHI SWA HA!**

> Master Quan's version: **GATE, GATE, POLOGATE, POLOSANGATE BODHI SWA HA!**

Kshitigarbha (Dizang, Jizo) Bodhisattva's name means *Earth Matrix* or *Earth Store*. He is the Bodhisattva who freely enters and leaves the hell worlds to liberate beings greatly suffering there. He is dressed as a traveling monk and carries a staff in his right hand and the chintamani, or wish-fulfilling mind gem, in his left. Kshitagarbha's mantra protects us against negativity from hell beings and hell worlds while extending our compassion to those experiencing the depths of intense suffering.

Traditional Sanskrit version: **AUM HA HA HA VISMAYE SWAHA!**

Master Quan's second-level version: **AUM PA RA MO RIN DU NING SO HA!**

White Tara is another aspect of Tara, the Liberator. Reciting this mantra leads to creation of auspicious conditions, improved health and longevity, prosperity for yourself and others, and accumulation of positive karma. One of the central causes of the devolution of society, depletion of Earth, and debasement of living beings is a lack of accumulated positive energy in our bodies, auras, and minds. This energy force in former times arose and grew from living life in harmony with nature and neighbors. It also arose from practicing virtue and internal transformational yogas. White Tara's mantra conserves and increases this store of positive energy for yourself and others so that we all may rise up.

Traditional Sanskrit version: **AUM TARE TUTTARE TURE MAMA AYUH PUNYA JNANA PUSHTIM KURU SWAHA!**

Master Quan's third-level version: **AUM DARE DWEI DARE DWEI LE MAMA_A YUINOH BUINA JAINA BEN JIN GURUYE SO HA!**

APPENDIX 2

Spiral Dragon Exercise Sequences

The following thumbnail presentations give a visual overview of each of the Spiral Dragon exercise sequences. The page numbers indicate where the exercise instructions can be found in the book.

Audio instructions for these exercises can be found at https://audio.innertraditions.com/spiraldragondharmagate/

Spiral Dragon Relax

See page 35 for a detailed description of this exercise.

Sky Dragon

See page 39 for a detailed description of this exercise.

Spiral Dragon Hands

See page 46 for a detailed description of this exercise.

Spiral Dragon Fingers

See page 51 for a detailed description of this exercise.

Spiral Dragon Palms

See page 54 for a detailed description of this exercise.

Spiral Dragon Meditation: Body Posture

See page 57 for a detailed description of this exercise.

Expelling Imbalanced Qi

See page 63 for a detailed description of this exercise.

Spiral Dragon Hand Mudras

See page 91 for a detailed description of this exercise.

 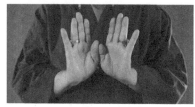

Pulsing Your Palms to Earth

See page 95 for a detailed description of this exercise.

Pulsing Your Palms to A Distant Object

See page 97 for a detailed description of this exercise.

Pulsing Energy for Healing

See page 99 for a detailed description of this exercise.

Appendix 2

Whole Hand Spiral Dragon Mudras: Contacting and Intensifying

See page 106 for a detailed description of this exercise.

Whole Hand Spiral Dragon Mudras: Receiving Energy and Information Passively

See page 109 for a detailed description of this exercise.

Whole Hand Spiral Dragon Mudras: Sending Energy and Information

See page 110 for a detailed description of this exercise.

Whole Hand Spiral Dragon Mudras: Life Torch Mudra

See page 111 for a detailed description of this exercise.

Spiral Dragon Sitting Posture

See page 68 for a detailed description of this exercise.

Performing Energetic Pause to Conserve Your Energy

See page 72 for a detailed description of this exercise.

Notes

Introduction to Spiral Dragon

1. Sessan, "Hakuin's 'Song of Meditation,'" in *A First Zen Reader*, 68.
2. Kaptchuk, *The Web That Has No Weaver: Understanding Chinese Medicine*, 78.
3. Holland, *Voices of Qi: An Introductory Guide to Traditional Chinese Medicine*, 22.
4. Ahn and Martinsen, "Electrical characterization of acupuncture points: technical issues and challenges," 817–24.

Chapter 3. Beginning Spiral Dragon

1. Leonhardt, *Fundamentals of Electroacupuncture According to Voll: An Introduction*.

Chapter 5. Restoring Your Health and Energy

1. Lao Tzu, *Lao Tzu's Taoteching*, 8.

Chapter 6. Creative Play and Progress

1. Davidson, *The Next End of the World*, 81–84.
2. SpaceWeatherLive, "Top Fifty Solar Flares."

Chapter 8. Mudra, Mantra, and Inner Transformation

1. Khenchen Lama Rinpoche, "Guru Rinpoche Mantra Mudra," YouTube, accessed January 11, 2024.

Epilogue

1. *The I Ching or Book of Changes*, 58.

Appendix I. Spiral Dragon Mantra Wisdom

1. Jayarava, *Visible Mantra*.

Bibliography

Ahn, Andrew C., and Orjan G. Martinsen. "Electrical characterization of acupuncture points: technical issues and challenges." *Journal of Alternative and Complementary Medicine* 13, no. 8 (2007): 817–24.

Davidson, Ben. *The Next End of the World*. Space Weather News, 2021.

Govert, Johndennis. *Feng Shui: Art and Harmony of Place*. Daikakuji Publications, 1993.

Govert, Anita, and Johndennis Govert. *Realty Feng Shui: Places and Profits in the Marketplace*. Zengo House, 2018.

Govert, Johndennis, and Hapi Hara. *The Chintamani Crystal Matrix: Quantum Intention and the Wish-Fulfilling Gem*. Destiny Books, 2022.

Holland, Alex. *Voices of Qi: An Introductory Guide to Traditional Chinese Medicine*. North Atlantic Books, 1999.

The I Ching or Book of Changes. Translated by Richard Wilhelm and Cary Baynes. Princeton University Press (third edition), 1967.

Jayarava. *Visible Mantra: Visualising and Writing Buddhist Mantras*. Visible Mantra Books, 2011.

Kaptchuk, Ted. *The Web That Has No Weaver: Understanding Chinese Medicine*. Congdon and Weed, 1983.

Khenchen Lama Rinpoche. "Guru Rinpoche Mantra Mudra." YouTube. Accessed January 11, 2024.

Lao Tzu. *Lao Tzu's Taoteching*. Translated by Red Pine. Mercury House, 1996.

Leonhardt, H. *Fundamentals of Electroacupuncture According to Voll: An Introduction*. ML Verlag, 1980.

Sessan, Amakuki. "Hakuin's 'Song of Meditation.'" In *A First Zen Reader*. Edited and translated by Trevor Leggett. Charles E. Tuttle Co, Inc., 1960.

SpaceWeatherLive. "Top Fifty Solar Flares." Website accessed December 31, 2024.

Index

accomplishments, 77–79
acupuncture, 126
adaptogenic quality, 62
AH, 113
altars, 33
audio recordings, 112, 153
AUM, 113–14
aura meridians, 25–26
awareness, 25, 28

back aches, 53, 91
bija, 144
bindus, 26–27, 126
black magic, 118–19
blessings, 82–83, *82*
Blue Beryl Medicine Buddha, 111
bodhicitta, 119–20
bodhi mind, 119–21, 125
Bodhisattvas, 119
bubbling spring, 65
Buddha, 13, 80, *131*, *132*
Buddhist Heart Sutra, 115

carbon monoxide, 15–16
cardinal directions, 84–85
chakras, 26
chintamani, 10, 135
circadian rhythms, 83–84
colds, 62

compassion, 4–5, 119, 120–21
confidence, 5
consciousness, 25, 27, 30–31, 34, 46, 116, 129

Daikakuji. *See* Great Enlightenment Temple
daily life, 41–42
dakini script, 18
Daoism, 15, 22
depletion, 69–74
destiny. *See* dharma
dharma, 10–11, 13, 88–91, 119, 134–38
disasters, 146–47
discomfort, 35–37, 38
distress, 80
DNA double helix structure, 7, *7*
do good, 124–25
dragon, meaning of character, 9–10

ears, 28
earthquakes, 88–89, 147
eclipses, 147
eight-word core dharma, 121–27
electroacupuncture test, 44
Energetic Pause, 71–74, *73*
Energy Body Qi Retrieval, 71–72
energy structures, 24–28, 30

enlightenment, 5–6, 9, 29–30, 33, 63
 hands and, 130–33
 many paths to, 13–14, 80
 restoring, 74–75
enso mudra, 43–44, *43*
ethereal bodies, 25
exercises
 Contacting and Intensifying, 106–8, *107, 108*
 Energetic Pause, 71–74, *73*
 Energy Body Qi Retrieval, 71–72
 Expelling Imbalanced Qi, 63–67, *64–65*
 Pulsing Your Palms to a Distant Object, 97–99, *98*
 Pulsing Your Palms to the Earth, 95–97, *96*
 Receiving Energy and Information Passively, 109
 Relax, 35–38, *36*
 Sending Energy and Information, 110–11, *110–11*
 Sky Dragon, 38–41, *40*
 Spiral Dragon Hands, 45–50, *47, 49*
 Spiral Dragon Palms, 53–55, *55, 78*
 Spiral Dragon Sitting Posture, 68–69, *69*
Expelling Imbalanced Qi, 63–67, *64–65*
experience fields, 42–44
eyebrows, 37
eyes, 28

feet, 28, 37
feng shui, 77, 97, 134
Fibonacci number sequence, 7
fingers. *See* Spiral Dragon Fingers
fire element, 25–26
five elements, 25

flexibility, 41–42
flu, 62
frequency, 24, 27
frustration, 36–37

gate, meaning of character, 11
generosity, 125
geography, 114
Govert, Johndennis
 dharma unfolding destiny, 134–38
 Master Quan and, 1–3, 102–3
 meditation and, 18
 mudras and, 102–3
 pictured, *21*
gratitude, 33
Great Enlightenment Temple, 21–22
Green Tara practice, 20, 147–48
gurus, 126
gushing spring, 37

HA, 112–13
Hakuin Ekaku, 6
hand mudras, *92*
hands, 28, 91–95, *92, 94*, 130–33
happiness, 24, 80
healing
 examples of, 89–91
 practicing Spiral Dragon, 61–63
 pulsing and, 99–101, *100*
 restoring enlightenment, 74–75
health, mantras for, 144–45
health extremes, 74
heart chakra, 28–29
Heart Sutra, 115
hormones, 26–27
Hsi Lai Temple, 88

ignorance, 1, 123
incense, 33
infinity symbol, 42–43, *43*
information, 31
inquiries, 96–97
insights, 78–79, 86–87
integration, 25
intention, 4–5, 33–34, 82–83, 119
intuition, 122

jing luo, 8–9

Kailash, Mount, 109
Kalachakra mandala, 137–38, *138*
karma, 14, 29–30, 63, 80, 125, 132–33
Khandro Senton Dorje, 31–32
  biography of, 14
  Master Quan and, 15–16
  pictured, *17*
  retreat cave of, 18–20, *19*
kiatsu therapies, 126
Kidney channel, 37
knees, 37
Koryo microsystem, 93, 132
Kumbun monastery, 17–19

lao gong, 48
liberation, path of, 5–6
life force flame mudra, 111, *111*
life purpose, 33
Life Torch Bodhi Temple, 83
light, 30–31
linear display, 9
linguistics, 113–14

Machig Labdron, 16, 23
magnetic attraction, 51, 53–54, 85
mahagurus, 126

mahasiddhas, 126
mahatmas, 126
Maitreya, 56
Mantrakaras, 115–16
mantras, 4, 71, 112–17
  Buddhist, 148–52
  for illness, 61–63
  pronunciation, 140–42
  repetitions of, 143–45
  Spiral Dragon, 144–48
  three modes of voicing, 142–43
  transmission and practice power, 140
  visualizations and, 143
Medicine Buddha, *131*, *132*
meditation, 42, 55–60, *58*, 77
  body posture, 57–58
  breath and breathing, 59
  meditative mind and thoughts, 59–60
men, 81
meridians, 25
merit, 125–27
Messier 83, *8*
method, path of, 5–9
microsystems, 93, 132
Milky Way, 7
mobius strip, 42–43, *43*
mothers, 146
mudras, 4, *92*, 103–11
  Contacting and Intensifying, 106–8, *107*, *108*
  enso, 43–44, *43*
  fields of sense information, 105–6
  hand, 91–93, *92*
  Receiving Energy and Information Passively, 109
  table of correspondences, 105

navel, 48, 51, 56, 59, 67–68, 73, 109
negative qi, 67
neidan, 123
ninety days, significance of, 79
NOAA, 85
Norbulingka, 136–37
Nyingma tradition, 14, 16, 17, 20, 23, 139

open practice system, 38
orbs, 26–27
outdoors, 83

pain, 35–37, 38
palms, 93–99, *94*
Pantanjali, 31
path of liberation, 5–6
path of method, 5–9
People's Republic of China (PRC), 2, 15
perfection, 6
play, 53, 54–55, 56, 60, 74, 78–79
pointed focus, 67–68
posture, for meditation, 57–58
Potala Palace, 135–36
practice
  cardinal directions, 84–85
  conditions for, 81
  engaging Spiral Dragon insight, 86–87
  exercise sequence, 153–59
  place and time of day, 82–84
  session length, 76–77
  signs of regress and progress, 127–30
  timeframes for accomplishments, 77–79
prayers, 33, 82–83
progress, signs of, 127–30

pull/release exercise, 51–53, 54, 59
pulsing, 95–101, *98*, *100*, 108

qi energy, 7–9, 25–26, 30–31, 63, 67–68
qi gong, 8–9
qi healing, 126–27
Quan, Guan-liang, 1–2, 31–32
  biographical information, 14–23
  black magic and, 118–19
  geologic stress and, 88–89
  healing abilities of, 89–91
  initiations and, 137
  learning Spiral Dragon, 16, 18, 20
  mantras and, 141–42
  meeting Senton Dorje, 16–20
  mudras and, 113, 115, 116–17
  perfecting Spiral Dragon, 22–23
  photos in shirt pocket, 20–23, *21*, *22*
  pictured, *19*, *21*
  quotes of, 1, 12
  sending wisdom and qi, 34
  sudden depletion and, 69–70
questions
  individual differences, 80
  place and time of day, 82–84
  practice conditions, 81
  session length, 76–77
  timeframes for accomplishments, 77–79

Red Guard, 17
regression, 127–30
regret misdeeds, 122
Relax, 27, 34–38, *36*, 129
release, 80
rice, cooking analogy, 77

Richter scale, 89
root mudra, *58*, 104

sacred languages, 114–15
Sanskrit, 114–15
Second Sino-Japanese War, 15
seed syllables, 144
self-acceptance, 28
self-healing, 61–63
self-involvement, 128
self-love, 28
self-perception, 28
session length, 76–77
Shambhala, 134–35
shoulder rotation, 49
siddhas, 126
siddhi, 126
sinking qi field, 97
sitting, 67–69
Sky Dragon, 34–35, 38–41, *40*, 129
sky dragons, 10
Solar Cycle 23, 86
solar system, 7
sounds, 37–38, 114–15
speech, 114–15
spine, 39–41, 91–93
spiral, meaning of character, 6
Spiral Dragon Dharma Gate. *See*
    exercises; practice; *specific topics*
Spiral Dragon Fingers, 50–53
Spiral Dragon Hands, 45–50, *47*, *49*, 128
Spiral Dragon Meditation, *58*
    body posture, 57–58
    breath and breathing, 59
    meditative mind and thoughts, 59–60
Spiral Dragon Palms, 53–55, *55*, 78
spiral dynamic, 38
spiritual practice, 5–9

spontaneous awareness, 6
standing, 67–68
stretching, 41
subsystems, 28
sudden depletion, 69–74
suffering, 91
swaying, 78

tantric Buddhism, 14, 16, 136, 151
tectonic stress, 89
terma, 14
terton, 14
thigles, 26–27
thumbs up, 111, *111*
Tibetan Buddhism, 14, 16, 26
time, bounds of, 29–30
timeframes, 77–79
tongue, 28
Traditional Chinese Medicine
    (TCM), 8, 14–15, 25
transfer merit, 125–27
transformation, 28–29, 30–32
transform inside, 123–24
tummo, 26

Voll, Reinhard, 44

water element, 25
women, 81
World War II, 15

yang energy, 53
yin energy, 53
yoga of fire, 120
Yoga Sutras, 31
yongquan, 65

Zazen Wasan, 6

BOOKS OF RELATED INTEREST

The Secret Fire of Alchemy
Kriya Yoga, Kundalini, and Shamanism
By Kevin B. Turner

Guided by a profound series of dream initiations, astral travels, and intense Kundalini activation, Kevin Turner embarks on an around-the-world quest in pursuit of the secret fire of alchemical enlightenment. He shares his initiations into Kriya Yoga and Tibetan Buddhism with high-level yogis and lamas and his discovery of parallels between Western Alchemy and Eastern traditions.

Flight of the Bön Monks
War, Persecution, and the Salvation of Tibet's Oldest Religion
By Harvey Rice and Jackie Cole

Providing an inside view into the occupation of Tibet and the tenets of Bön, one of the world's oldest but least known religions, this book chronicles the true story of three Bön monks who heroically escaped occupied Tibet during the Chinese invasion and went on to rebuild their culture through incredible resilience, determination, and passion.

Kriya Yoga for Self-Discovery
Practices for Deep States of Meditation
By Keith G. Lowenstein, M.D., with Andrea J. Lett, M.A.

Offering an accessible guide to Kriya yoga, Keith Lowenstein, M.D., explains the basic techniques of the practice step by step, detailing proper posture, breathwork exercises (pranayama), visualization practices, and mantra. He reveals how Kriya is a scientific art—if practiced consistently, it will allow you to quickly enter deep states of meditation.

Scan the QR code and save 25% at InnerTraditions.com. Browse over 2,000 titles on spirituality, the occult, ancient mysteries, new science, holistic health, and natural medicine.

— SINCE 1975 • ROCHESTER, VERMONT —

InnerTraditions.com • (800) 246-8648